SAILING:

A Parent's Guide to Junior Sailing

2nd Edition

SAILING:

A Parent's Guide to Junior Sailing

2nd Edition

by
Susan Artof

The Center Press
PO Box 6936
Thousand Oaks, CA 91362
(818) 889-7071
Fax (818) 889-7072
www.centerbooks.com

Sailing: A Parent's Guide to Junior Sailing by Susan D. Artof

Copyright © 1994by Susan D. Artof   2nd Edition 2002

1st Edition 1994   ISBN 0-9626888-3-5
2nd Edition 2002   ISBN 1-889198-09-9

Published by:
The Center Press P.O. Box 6936 Thousand Oaks, CA 91360-6936

Publisher's Cataloging-in-Publication Data
    Artof, Susan D. 1949-
    Sailing: a parent's guide to junior sailing / by Susan Dale Artof
    p.cm. — (Boating made simple)
    Includes bibliographical references and index.
    Preassigned LCCN
    ISBN 1-889198-09-9
    1. Sailing. I. Title

Photos by Virginia Howard
Cover and interior design by Lindsay Artof
Illustrations by Lindsay Artof
Edited by Susan D. Artof & Lindsay Artof
Printed by T/O Printing

Printed and bound in the United States of America
10 9 8 7 6 5 4 3 2

Dedication

To Del Rey Yacht Club, Westlake Yacht Club, and the entire Santa Monica Bay Sailing Community for all of their support of junior sailing during the past twenty-eight years.

A special thank you to Virginia Howard for her many years of dedicated service to the junior community in Southern California. Her special brand of compassion has influenced hundreds of young sailors and helped change their lives for the better. I am grateful to her for the use of the photographs I have chosen to use in this book. They have helped bring life to these pages.

Contents

Introduction

Sailing is perhaps one of the last remaining pure freedoms left in a complicated world. It is the type of recreational activity that is spiritually and physically healthy for children of all ages. Probably because we are nurtured from water, we happily return to the water when given a chance. A child finds new adventure each time he or she rigs up a boat and sets sail on even the smallest body of water. Sailing allows the child to harness the wind and take flight on a vessel with no restraining lines in the road or sidewalks to navigate. It is that very freedom to be in touch with the essence of nature that is so incredibly exhilarating for both children and adults. The sport is clean, exciting and it teaches self-reliance. Sailing knows only the limitations of the vessel and the skipper. However, water presents continually new challenges to our senses and our sensibilities, and it is always important to remain alert when returning to it.

I wrote my first book titled *Sailing: A Parent's Handbook For Junior Sailing* because of my own experience as a parent watching my two children grow up around junior sailing programs learning about the special world of sailing. I've updated the original book with this second book on *Sailing: A Parent's Guide To Junior Sailing* as a result of working with sailing programs and other parents for more than 25 years. My husband and I have listened to countless parents discuss their children's sporting activities such as tee-ball, soccer and baseball. Most parents have experienced these sports themselves as children, and they can easily find a field or backyard on any given day of the week to practice with their kids. If they do not physically throw a ball, parents can comfortably sit in bleachers and cheer their young players forward, knowing that a coach is present to accelerate skills and strategy. Unlike these sports, sailing presents a unique problem for parents since many of them have never learned to sail themselves and often feel alienated from the activity. Instead, they rely on what the sailing instructor might send home with the child at the end of the day. For example, although there is a common vocabulary in sailing which sailors seem to understand (although, don't fool yourself—many do not), most non sailors have no idea what the terms mean. *Boomvang, centerboard, bailer, batten or clew* are all common words used out on the water. But, when a child comes home the first day of sailing class to report that his friend was sailing a *flying junior* whose *foot* tore on the last leg of the *luff-in*, an unknowing parent might think a catastrophe occurred and call an ambulance. What really happened was that his friend was sailing a two person type of boat called a flying junior and tore the bottom part of the sail called the foot in the last part of a race called a luff-in. Sounds easy when you know what you are listening to. It sounds like a foreign language when you don't.

As parents struggle to understand the vocabulary of the young sailor, they run the risk of misunderstanding their children's needs. Children will commonly ask their parents for advice or help, and their parents are unable to effectively give it to them. As equipment breaks and tempers soar on both sides, the words turn to demands and they become heated. I have heard children shouting at their parents to bring them boat or sail parts while the parents stand mutely in the parking lot fuming over the humiliation of an 8 year old barking out commands like a Navy commander. This behavior is definitely out of line! Conversely, parents are equally guilty of shouting out commands to their kids that are just not developmentally appropriate. Not all kids are able to sail with the same degree of skill at the same time of their life. While one 10 year old may win a fleet championship, the other is happy as can be sailing around in circles. Parents should not expect more from their kids then is realistic. So it is with this need for greater communication in mind that I considered the importance of writing a book directed to parents about the world of sailing at the junior/youth level.

As both a past educator in psychology and a parent of a national champion youth sailor, I understand the importance of communication with children. A child's self esteem depends upon a clear sense of boundaries and values as well as a certain amount of success at something he or she is good at. The more a parent understands about the child's world, the better the communication of these values and boundaries can be and the more pleasure the child can get from their success. Children who do not have a strong sense of self worth may often thrash around their social world and lash out for attention somewhere. In other words, these children may find themselves getting into more and more trouble with both adults and their own peers. It is imperative that children learn how to handle their stresses in productive and appropriate ways and not turn to violence or performance enhancing substances which can only lead to disaster. For this reason, I have included chapters on sportsmanship, sports psychology along with chapters on equipment needs and vocabulary. It is also important that parents understand what to look for in a quality program and I have included a chapter detailing the elements of such a program.

I have asked several experts in their area to write chapters in this book in order to enhance information that makes this book especially useful to parents and sailing program developers. These people have been selected for their specialty and asked to write chapters focusing on junior sailing. Readers may find it helpful to use these chapters as an introduction to the subject matter, and find other books that cover the information in greater depth.

Claudia Wainer, M.A. is clinically trained in psychology and has specialized in the area of *Sports Psychology and child welfare.* She is a champion sailor on both large and small boats, giving her specific understanding of what unique stresses occur during competition on the water. We have asked her to write a chapter in this book on *Sports Psychology specifically designed towards young sailors.*

Chris Camacho currently works in sports management and is completing his Master's degree at the University of San Francisco. For several years, he was a personal physical sports trainer specializing in personal fitness training for people of all ages. Chris writes about some of the special physical training necessary to help avoid injury and maximize strength when competing. He communicates his unique understanding of specific sports needs in his chapter titled *Fitness For Kids.*

Paul Artof is an SCYA trained Principal Race Officer and a past Race Committee Chairman of Del Rey Yacht Club and Commodore of Westlake Yacht Club. He has been active both on the water and in race management for more than 25 years. Paul has contributed a chapter in this book on *Race Course Procedure* to help parents understand the often complex horns, time sequences and flags which all racing sailors must eventually become comfortable with.

Jason Artof, 27, is a trained **US SAILING** Instructor and has sailed in junior programs since he was 7 1/2 years old. He has traveled throughout the United States and Japan, competing in national and international level races, winning the doublehanded Bemis Trophy at the *USYRU-Rolex Junior Championships* (this race is now known as the **US SAILING**/*Rolex Junior Championships*) in 1989. He was selected as a member of the first Youth Rolex Sailing Team. Today he is a biomechanical engineer and in his sparetime teaches sailing at the UC Irvine sailbase. He brings first hand information about what it is like to instruct young sailors and specifically, what parents might do to enhance their children's experience.

This book is intended to act as a reference guide for those parents who desire more for their child than just a simple summer class. I have devoted an entire chapter to sailing organizations including the national organization and governance body called **US SAILING Association**, located in Newport Rhode Island. **US SAILING** is responsible for developing the educational, racing, and training programs for all American sailors, young and old alike. From my experience as a parent of both high school and college sailors, I have included a discussion of the scholastic national and regional organizations that promote the sport of sailing. Finally, I have included information about yacht clubs and boat clubs that may be useful to readers who are considering becoming more involved with the sport and who may want to benefit from club membership for their family. There is no question that sailing can become a lifestyle in addition to a recreational sport. This book may help to illustrate some of the features of that lifestyle.

This book is not intended to teach anyone how to sail. There are several wonderful books on the market that cover boat mechanics and seamanship. In addition, a good community based sailing program can be helpful in achieving covering the basic sailing skills for relatively little money. However, it is my hope that readers might gain a further appreciation of the sport of sailing through increased understanding and awareness of what lies beneath the surface. Further, and even more important to me, is the hope that parents might actually increase their enjoyment of watching their child. Whether you continue to become involved in this sport is not nearly as critical as becoming more involved in your child's world. After all, they do have something quite magical to teach us.

Susan Artof

CHAPTER ONE
WHAT TO EXPECT

Today, children are given an opportunity to explore and experience so many more recreational activities than they were able to even a few years ago. It is not unusual for a child to play a different sport each season and maintain a practice schedule of three days per week while still in early elementary school. Football, baseball, soccer, basketball and even tennis all compete for your child's attention and time. Many parents I met while my children were growing up, spent almost every Saturday and most Sundays carpooling their offspring from one game to another, and if there were two or more children playing sports, then the entire family was separated across town.

The truth is, not every child is good at every sport, and some children do not perform well at team sports in any predictable way. Yet, each child has a right to be good at something, and it is each parent's responsibility to help his or her child navigate through the smorgasbord of choices available. Athletics teach children valuable lessons about life such as winning and losing, sportsmanship and confidence. Children with favorable athletic experiences, and this does not mean just winning, develop greater self acceptance and self esteem. Children having negative experiences in competition, which usually include unreasonable coaching or parental expectation, end up losing more then just games or races. They may lose the willingness to compete in a fair game. These children may cheat, lie or just give up. As parents help their children come up with those special gold nuggets of experiences that stretch their talents, they must also add ingredients to their children's confidence. Knowing what the sport is all about, and what it demands of its participants, adds to the positive experiences children and their parents get from recreational activities. So, let us examine what sailing as a sport, both recreational and competitive, is all about.

Recreational Sailing:

Beginning sailing for kids is considered a personal rather than a group oriented activity, even though classes are sometimes conducted on large boats with many people aboard. Sailing classes are usually structured around a group of 20 to 30 sailors, each assigned to a personal boat rigged with only one sail called the mainsail. The most common training boats are approximately 7 1/2 to 8 1/2 feet long and there are several different types (classes) of boats used in programs throughout the country. In Southern California, for example, we use several versions of a boat called a *Sabot*. *El Toros* and a homemade boat called a *Seashell* are often sailed in Northern California. The *Optimist*, the most popular class in the world, is used in many other areas of the country (classes of boats sailed throughout the country will be discussed in **Chapter 4**). What makes all of these boats particularly advantageous for training, is that they are light weight and easy to rig with only one sail to adjust which make it easier for the student sailor to learn the most effective way to harness the wind to power their vessel forward (hopefully). Once the skipper has learned to rig and sail their small single person vessel, they begin to master certain *rules of the road* dictating who may get the right of way when two or more boats meet. Although there are no lines in the water or stop signs at any intersection, boat handling does require a keen knowledge of these special rules in order to avoid disastrous and often embarrassing collisions. As these rules become mastered and fine tuned, the sailor learns other rules which may give him/her an advantage on a race course.

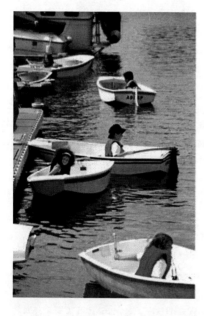

Learning to steer without a sail helps new kids getting comfortible in their boats on the first day of sailing classes.

When the sailor has completed a beginning course, and perhaps even an intermediate course of sailing, he/she may choose to sail a boat with more speed and excitement. They may choose a larger and faster single person boat (singlehanded) such as a *Laser* or *Sunfish* or they may chose to sail some of the exciting two handed (doublehanded) boats which many programs supply such as a *Club/Collegiate Flying Junior (CFJ)*, *Laser II* or *Club/Collegiate 420*. These boats are rigged with two sails, a *main* and a *jib*. Sometimes they also make use of a special sail called a *spinnaker*—the colored balloon type sail seen in photographs of sailboat races. People may choose to sail doublehanded (two people) in recreational areas such as at resorts or marinas, or they may begin to compete heavily in the local or national regatta circuit. The choice is up to the families involved. Even though 10-15% of junior sailors become racing skippers, the other 85% to 90% are happy sailing on a Sunday afternoon without worrying about any start or finish lines, race committee instructions or protests.

Finally, young and old sailors alike usually graduate to even larger boats and learn about real seamanship after they can sail in the harbor on smaller vessels. Such skills may include radio usage, medical emergency at sea requirements, navigation, boat handling in heavy weather, and offshore racing. Once a sailor enters this level of sailing, there is no end to the information that can be learned. Sailing is definitely a lifelong recreational activity which goes far beyond the early first lesson on the water. For example, one of the finest American sailors is Dennis Connor, who originally started his illustrious career sailing as a junior sailor in San Diego Yacht Club's Junior Program. He competed in almost every level of racing, finally culminating in the highest honor of international boat racing by winning the America's Cup. In 1993 he began training for the Around the World Race, then called the Whitbred Race, to be sailed in 1994. When asked why he wanted to encounter the hardships and difficulty of this particular race when he had already achieved the highest honor in racing, he answered that it remains important to him to continue developing his skills as a sailor. So it appears that sailing skills are never fully mastered but only improved over time.

From a Sabot to a large boat takes some time but is a lifelong pleasure.

Competitive Sailing:

During early training, young sailors experience the excitement of personal mastery over equipment and nature without the worry of team mate expectation. In fact, it is quite possible to spend most of one's sailing time in non competitive recreation which makes sailing quite unique when compared to soccer, football, or basketball. However, sailing programs usually begin to acquaint skippers with racing activities soon into the session as a way to reinforce certain boat handling skills. Children seem to enjoy working on efforts to maximize their equipment to go faster, and racing allows them to test success against others in the class. Because sailboat racing allows each individual skipper to test their own skills, sailing provides a specific niche for those who find it difficult or uncomfortable playing team sports. There are no pre-chosen positions to play in sailboat racing, and each child is given an equal chance to play the game and feel that they are in control of the situation.

We will take up the specifics of sailboat racing in another chapter, but for now, it should be mentioned that not all children like the win loss orientation of certain structured sailing programs, and it is important for parents to discuss with their child what winning and losing is all about. Many children come home tired and cranky from a day of sailing because it is hard work even though it is fun. Children may feel upset that they lost every race that day or that their equipment broke. They may ask you to go back to the program and tell the instructors not to place so much emphasis on racing skills. Yet, these kids are still learning valuable lessons beyond just winning a race or sailing the fastest. They are learning something important about themselves in an atmosphere of support from trained instructors. Parents may want to take an opportunity to discuss exactly what is bothering the child and help that child cope with the hard work rather then giving up. It is not as important that they win, but that they attempt to win. Even by losing once in awhile, children learn something about their limitations and strengths.

As sailing skills increase, young sailors may chose to become specialized as either a driver (or skipper) or crew (boat handler or tactician). The two person boat like the *29er, International One Design 14, Flying Junior (CFJ), Laser II,* or *420* all require strong and supportive teamwork between skipper and crew. Oftentimes, the crew is chosen because of weight or size requirements, and may be an excellent driver in addition to boat handler. Further, the skipper may be more experienced as a crew, but because of certain physical requirements of the particular boat being sailed, must act as driver for the afternoon. It is necessary that the skipper and crew respect each other, and neither position should treat the other as a lesser participant in the race. I have watched crew and skipper

A 29er with its spinnaker flying and crew hiked out.

Close racing on the course requires teamwork, especially on trapeze boats such as the 420.

fights which have left both children emotionally injured for no other reason then disrespect for what each bring to the race. Teamwork eventually becomes essential to the sport, and parents might encourage communication between both parties. In addition, skipper parents should treat the crew parents with as much respect as the actual teammates. Many regattas today will make an effort to recognize both the winning crew and skipper with trophies and publicity. But, this is not always the case, and in certain regattas, only the skipper is recognized. Feelings may be further hurt when a crew and family work hard to achieve a winning attitude only to be forgotten by the skipper and family. It is important to consider crewed boats as a team since the boat cannot be sailed by just one person. Everyone becomes a part of the action!

Scholastic Sailing: College and High School
Collegiate Sailing:
The governing organization of collegiate sailing in the United States is called the Inter-Collegiate Sailing Assiciation (ICSA). It is comprised of more than 200 sailing clubs and teams organized into seven Districts: Middle Atlantic Intercollegiate Sailing Association (MAISA); Midwest College Association (MCSA); New England Intercollegiate Sailing Association (NEISA); Northwest Intercollegiate Yacht Racing Association (NWIYRA); Pacific Coast Intercollegiate Yacht Racing Association (PCIYRA); South Atlantic Intercollegiate Sailing Association (SAISA); South Eastern Intercollegiate Sailing Association (SEISA).

Each district manages its own local and intersectional events leading up to a District Championship. Winners from this continue on to the North American Championships.

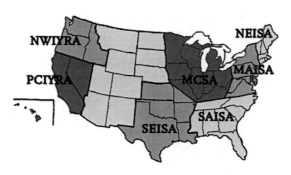

ICSA Member Districts

What is unique about many of the collegiate programs is that they make it a point to develop training and educational programs for members of their community and in some cases, the public at large. ICSA has made it part of their mission to conduct these classes since collegiate sailing began in the 1890's. The following college and university programs are specifically designed to increase the skills of the recreational sailing community

MIT
University of Wisconsin-Madison
College Of Charleston
University Of California Irvine

At the collegiate level, a full sailing team or program may consist of just a few sailors or as many as twenty or thirty, however, only one representative from each entered fleet, may actually be scored in a regatta. Usually at any college sailing event, there will be an A fleet team and a B fleet team represented for each such fleet. Therefore, even though your child may be on the sailing team, only the top level four or six people may be allowed to sail in a doublehanded event and as few as two people may be asked to sail in a singlehanded event. However, all teammates are expected to practice between three and five times per week whether they are active regatta sailors or not.

As a side note, it is not uncommon for a rock star or local champion in high school to enter the college scene with hopeful dreams of becoming an All American, yet be placed on the "inactive" practice squad for the first year while he/she learns the hard lesson of how college sailing differs from club sailing. Sometimes a sailing team's practice schedule may actually interfere with the academic courses the sailor is taking. It is important for the collegiate sailor to keep his/her education a high priority.

The most commonly used boats in college sailing are Lasers for the singlehanded races and Flying Juniors or 420s for the doublehanded events. Boats are rotated through the competition so that any given team cannot win by their equipment alone since every other competitor will get a chance to sail the best and the worst boats. Courses are intentionally short so as to maximize the number of races each day. It is common for 10-15 or even more short races to be sailed during any college regatta.

It is important to note here that as of this writing, there are no scholarships allowed to be offered for college sailing. This is designed to protect the various sailing programs from going on a raiding campaign to recruit the few great college sailors to their program with offers of money. Certain programs are poorly funded while others maintain a war chest of several hundreds of thousands of dollars. Yet, almost every major sailing school can boast of a few nationally ranked sailors on their teams. What happens is that these programs will go off and recruit team members by promising a more relaxed admissions standard. A sailor should choose the campus they want to attend and then look into the sailing program. Good teams will look for good sailors. Small teams will look for sailors. And schools with no team may not

care at all. I am including a partial list of colleges which
have been listed in the *Sailing World Magazine* as pos-
sessing a varsity ranked sailing team. Contact the athletic
department at any of the schools listed and ask for information about how they recruit.

Boston U	Old Dominion
Brown	Princeton
California State U San Diego	Radcliff
Charleston	St. Marys
Coast Guard	Stanford
Conn. College	Tufts
Dartmouth	Tulane
Georgetown	U of Hawaii
Harvard	U of Rhode Island
King's Point	UC Berkeley
MIT	UC Irvine
Navy	UC Santa Barbara
New York Maritime	USC
Northwestern	Yale

In the 2002 college sailing issue of *Sailing World
Magazine*, the following schools were considered up and
coming schools for collegiate programs.:
U of Maryland at Baltimore County
U of South Florida
UC San Diego
Bowdoin College

Some of the favorite places college students like to sail are:
Lake Mendota - U of Wisconsin
Boca Ciega Bay - Eckart College
Lake Travis - University of Texas
Lake Masoma - Dartmouth College
St. Mary's River - St. Mary's College of Maryland

Finally, as a word of advice from someone who has paid the tuition and found that college is not a free ride to anyone. Coaches may not appreciate the philosophy that school comes before sailing (especially since there is no money in college sailing). A student has only four years of eligibility in any athletic sport including sailing. It is in no one's interest to poke around the campus just to sail the boat - not when a year at the cheapest campus can run $15,000 and an expensive one upwards to $32,000-$40,000. Therefore, sometimes students will be forced to **red shirt** or stop sailing for a semester if their schedules make it impossible for them to participate. Such red shirting is usually allowed from time to time, and a student/sailor might pick and chose what semesters they want to participate the most. The national championships are always sailed in the Spring for example making this the most desired semester to remain on the team.

For more information regarding ICSA or any college program, contact the President or District Graduate Secretary or the overall Graduate Secretary.

ICSA (Secretary)- 2002

CDR Eric Wallischeck, USMS
Yocum Sailing Center
U. S. Merchant Marine Academy
Kings Point, NY 11024-1699
o 516-773-5232
h 516-773-5770,
Fax 516-773-5344.
Or go online at
http://www.collegesailing.org

High School Sailing
High school sailing is the fastest growing part of youth sailing and is quite popular as high schools begin to

accept the sport as a varsity activity. Like the colleges, there are seven districts in high school sailing. Eligibility begins at the ninth grade for sailors in both public and private schools. The active districts include Northeast (NESSA), Mid-Atlantic (MASSA), South Atlantic (SAISA), Southeast (SEISA), Midwest (MWISSA), Pacific Coast (PCISA), and Northwest (NWISA).

High School sailing allows for social time on the beach between races.

High school sailing is run very much like the college sport with A and B fleets participating at each regatta. However, there is more room for interpretation of regatta structure at each high school event. Parents and juniors should not hesitate to ask their principals or athletic directors if such a program is something which can be developed in the local region. Coaches are often recruited from the colleges and often times clubs will help to donate boats or launching ramps for this activity. For more information regarding high school sailing contact the:

Interscholastic Sailing Association (ISSA)
> Larry White, President
> PO Box 397
> Niantic, CT 06357
> (203) 739-3253

Or Contact **US SAILING** direct at
> (401) 849-5200
> Or go to the web at
> *http://www.highschoolsailingusa.org*

The three major national High School Championships are as follows:

Cressy Cup: National singlehanded Championship-One Person from a high school may qualify through a district championship elimination.

Mallory Cup: National Doublehanded Team Championships - Named after Clifford Mallory who was the commodore of Indian Harbor Yacht Club in 1930 when the first high school championship was established. Like the Cressy, this event selects the top teams from district championships. A minimum 4 person team from the same High School competes with an A and a B division participating.

Baker Cup: National Team Racing Championships. This event is named after Toby Baker of Tabor Academy. Toby helped make scholastic sailing more professional with his program designed to develop sailing coaches. A Baker team is comprised of a minimum of 6 sailors from the same high school. Sailors compete in a three boat team on the water at the same time sailing against another team of three boats, with a combined team best score advancing. Twelve winners of district eliminations compete in the championship rotated throughout the country each year.

CHAPTER TWO
PROGRAM QUALITY

Local and national sailing organizations meet each year to discuss program quality issues and develop ways to improve the way sailing is taught to children and adults. The dialog and written information at these meetings is invaluable, and I have learned that there are great similarities between programs, even if some are bigger than others. Eight of the most important criteria used to create a great program and evaluate a program's quality are:

1) Parent involvement
2) Instructor child ratio
3) Staff training
4) Equipment
5) Effective emergency procedures
6) An organized plan and curriculum
7) Staff ability to be child sensitivity
8) Zero drug and alcohol tolerance.

Parent Involvement:

The best advice I can give parents who are deciding where to send their child for recreation, is to become as educated as possible about the way that program is administered. This is true whether it a sailing, football, soccer or an art class. However, unlike many sports like baseball or tennis, sailing is not an activity that is well understood by non-sailors. In fact, sailing is a sport that appears to keep outsiders away by the fact that a when a sailor goes out on the water, people on shore cannot view them. Further, as I discuss in **Chapter 3**, sailing uses a special vocabulary reserved for those in the know. Outsiders are vulnerable to feeling alienated and uncomfortable. I have been to many parent child meetings where parents sit outside the main circle of participants and read the Sunday paper rather than projecting any opinions on how to make the program better. I cannot stress enough how important it is for parents to become an active part of their child's activity, even going as far as getting in a boat themselves and trying it out!

Parents make the docks bow as they watch the racing from the docks

Learn How To Rig A Boat Yourself:
Parents who drop their children off at the sailing program, only to reappear several hours later, are often bewildered about their child's fears and concerns or even discipline problems. Further, these parents are rarely able to anticipate equipment needs and often the missing or broken equipment causes a child to have a "bad" day in the program. The more successful young sailors usually have a

parent or two nearby and somewhat available during the day. Even with the working schedules for many families, a parent can either help with their child's boat in the morning or at the end of the day. Furthermore, they might choose to work with their child on the water after program hours.

Look for a program that includes extra activities for parents to learn something about the sport. Most programs, whether large or small, will offer activities for parents to become involved in their child's program. At Del Rey Yacht Club in Marina Del Rey and Westlake Yacht Club in Westlake Village, we host evening activities several times per week and encourage parents to come by and watch their children sail. The main purpose is to encourage parental involvement and communication. In addition, the increased social interaction between parents and instructors help reduce some of the anxiety for both the parent and the child.

Get In The Boat And Sail:
At Del Rey Yacht Club in Marina Del Rey, I learned first hand how important it was to get on (and sometimes in) the water with your own child. When my first child began to sail at age 7 1/2, I found that on any given morning, there were parents "hanging" around the docks helping to rig up the rather heavy and cumbersome Sabots (8 foot sailboats) in the program. In those days, the program made it mandatory that a *Parent of the Day* (POD) be available to help instructors with some of the routine daily problems that occurred. In addition to this POD, Wednesday mornings became special as the women of the marina, including members from several local yacht clubs, took to their own boats to sail along with their children. Some of the children actually rigged up their personal boats to loan to their mothers for the morning. That made it definitely easier to sail!

I was one of those Wednesday mothers, sailing along in my small boat, often feeling quite out of control. What made this time particularly meaningful to me, was that my child was able to watch me struggle with the very activity he was trying to learn. It gave him added confidence in his own abilities. I may have been older, but he was infinitely more agile and coordinated than me. This became abundantly clear on one particular Saturday when he and I were both racing our Sabots in the SCYA Midwinter Regatta. We had turned towards the finish line, sailing neck and neck, with our boats crashing through the waves (well, maybe there were no waves...only little ripples...but to me they seemed like waves at the time). I was convinced that I was ahead of him until he caught a special gust of wind and sailed on ahead, leaving me eating his spray in the background. What did he do then? He just looked back at me with the widest grin I had ever seen and said, "Good race Mom." All I could feel was pride in his accomplishment. He had beaten a bigger and faster and more skilled parent. I obviously had nothing left to teach him in racing. There are few recreational activities where a youngster can out perform their parent by age 10 years of age! To help parents understand what it is like to sail a small boat, today, at Del Rey Yacht Club, we conduct a special Junior-Senior race for parents to compete with their kids just so that they can experience some of this pleasure — or pain for themselves.

At Westlake Yacht Club, parents are encouraged to come down to the club docks on Thursday nights after the end of a beginning sailing week of sailing. Before and after dinner, they get in a boat and learn some sailing from their kids. This is a casual activity with no racing. It is a hands on back to basics time for parents and their kids to relate to each other.

Ratio of Staff To Student:

Programs with the best reputations make it a point to staff themselves with enough personnel to maintain safety and security at all times. Although some programs feel that beginners and advanced sailors can sail together and help with some of the staffing problems, it is recommended that there is more staff for beginning sailors then for advanced ones. Good programs makes an attempt to use a ratio of:

   1 staff member for every 5 beginning sailors.
   1 staff member for every 8 intermediate sailors.
   1 staff for every 10 advanced sailors.

Various programs maintain different ratios. It is important to ask how many students are enrolled and how many staff are expected to be available each day, and then ask what the general mix of sailing skills will be within the overall program. Remember, beginners take more time and require more personal staff attention then the advanced sailors do. Consider your child's special needs when picking a program.

The staff is usually made up of a Head Instructor along with several Regular Instructors and some Assistant Instructors. The total number of staff depends upon the size of the program. For 10 sailors, there may be only two instructors. For a program of 15-20, there may be three or four instructors. If the program is 25-30 at least five instructors and perhaps some trainees called CITs (Counselor In Training) may be expected. Use your judgment and ask questions regarding the staffing of the program you are most interested in.

Staff Training:

There are special Instructor Training Certification programs that sailing instructors are encouraged to take before they are hired by most quality programs. These programs have been developed by professional sailing organizations to help increase the professional nature of the sport. The training I am most familiar with to help develop instructors, is the training program administered by **US SAILING Association**.

For more information regarding this National Governing Organization see *http://www.ussailing.org*.

The first level (*Small Boat Sailing Level 1*) of instructor training begins with a comprehensive four day 40 hour program designed to teach on the water group management skills. Sailing instructors are taught safety drills, use of the safety boat, sports psychology and physiology, lesson and curriculum planning, unique teaching techniques for the classroom and on the water, legal issues including risk management, as well as other safety considerations. Instructors apply with a resume of good sailing and powerboat handling skills in place. Successful passing of this class offers a valuable certification that must be kept up throughout the instructor's career.

The next level (*Small Boat Racing Level 2*) course emphasizes instruction on how to coach beginning and performance racing strategies. This 3-day course offers instructors a chance to build upon their mandatory Level 1 experience and prepare them to actually become on the water coaches. Coaches learn how to develop racing skills using a variety of on the water drills and demonstrations and off the water lectures to help the sailor develop a strong racing background. Instructors will be shown ways to demonstrate the physics of hydrodynamics of the hull, keel and rudder and the aerodynamics of the sail in order to maximize boat speed. A full day is devoted to boat-specific rigging and tuning. Both Level 1 and Level 2 require a rigorous in class and on the water performance standard that is tested before certification is given.

A **Windsurfing Instructor Course** is also offered in order to teach communication and sailing skills to those who desire to instruct beginning windsurfing. This 4-day program uses **US SAILING** designed material and focuses on how to increase on the water safety for windsurfers of all ages.

US SAILING also offers instruction for *Basic Keel Boat Instructors* (a 3-day evaluation for the most experienced teachers). A 3-day *Cruising and Coastal Navigation Instructor Course* has been developed to evaluate those who want to focus attention and skill on Bareboat Cruising and Navigation. Another sophisticated class has been recently developed to evaluate *Coastal Passage Making Instructors* during a 5-day course.

For those instructors who would like to learn how to train other instructors, **US SAILING** has developed a *Basic Keelboat Instructor Training class.* This 4-day course certifies instructors to become even more expert in their field so that they can help **US SAILING** develop a full curriculum of instruction for any and all levels of sailing.

The *Head Instructor,* of any quality program, should have a minimum of *Level 1* training plus several years of teaching all levels of sailing. All other Instructors and Assistant Instructors should also have the minimum *Level 1* course completed or be in the process of such training. Today, insurance companies are using the amount and quality of instructor training as part of the risk assessment when rating the policies of sailing programs and clubs. Although, no amount of training can absolutely assure against all accidents, **US SAILING** Instructor Training can help minimize the potential for such problems and assure some standard of quality in instruction.

Along with a minimum of Level 1 training, make sure that all of the staff is Red Cross Certified for CPR and First Aid. This is mandatory for **US SAILING**

Certification, but you may find some staff who are not certified Level 1. Be sure to ask if they are at least CPR and First Aid certified.

Equipment:
Keep in mind that there are small and large sailing programs, and depending upon the size, certain equipment for sailing may or may not be available. For example, some programs provide boats and life jackets while others request the student to provide their own boat. Some programs may have an onsite pool for swimming and even a snack bar for lunch. Others are community based programs located directly on the waterfront with few frills often found at a yacht club. However, regardless of size, there is little excuse for a lack of safety equipment. It is important that a program maintain the following equipment at all times:

1. A well stocked and usable first aid kit (**See Chapter 8: Fitness For Kids for a list of the bare minimum for such a kit**), located in several places throughout the area where your child may be sitting or sailing. Look for this in areas including:
   A. In the classroom or instruction area
   B. At the pool with the lifeguard
   C. Out on the water in at least one chase boat with each group

2. An adequate number of working chase boats or patrol boats and staff working with each group of sailors. These can be small 12-15 foot power boats (the Boston Whaler™ is a common boat of choice for this purpose) with strong motors. It is preferable that there is a chase boat for each sailing group that goes out on the water so that if there is a beginning group and an advanced group sailing in the afternoon, the program should provide two chase boats. If there are

three levels sailing, then there should be three boats patrolling. Sometimes, different skill levels may share a chase boat if they remain in the same general area, but it is hard to maintain order when too few chase boats are available, especially if the different skill levels begin to spread out on the water.

There should always be two instructors in each boat so that one can drive while one can assist in rescues. These boats should have motors that are well maintained and always working. In addition, adequate floatation devices should be aboard for all passengers. Finally, instructors should not take students aboard these boats for fun, and should only use them when conducting actual classes. Failure to follow this rule could jeopardize the entire program with the Coast Guard since drivers of boats with passengers may be required to have a Coast Guard License to carry passengers.

3. An adequate number of radios or communication devices such as telephones available both on and off the water. It is sometimes necessary to quickly contact an adult on the dock, especially if the program is conducted far away from the shore. A marine type radio or other two way radio, is very important. In some harbors, sailors may be three or more miles away from their home base, and immediate communication ability is essential for safety.

4. Enough blackboards for the instructors to use when gathering their students for the morning and afternoon chalk talks. These talks are an instructor's only way of communicating valuable information to each student before they actually go out on the water to practice.

5. Enough loud hailers for each instructor to call out instructions on the water. There should be enough

batteries available to keep these hailers working at all times.

6. Is there shade available if the sun is too strong? Is there some extra emergency sunscreen available if the child forgets to bring their own?

7. Are there lockers or spaces available for safe keeping of personal objects such as lunches or spending money?

A Well Designed Emergency Plan:

An emergency plan should include a signed medical release that is available to the program supervisors and instructors at all times your child is on the premises or traveling to and from a regatta or other related activity. This means that even when your child is traveling to regattas and you are not there, an adult should have a copy of your medical release available in case of an emergency. Besides giving *authorization for emergency medical treatment*, these forms should include *the name of your doctor*, the *preferred hospital* if available, *your insurance policy number* and of course *any allergic medical problems or unusual medical needs. The form must be signed and dated for it to be valid.*

Most clubs or community programs go to great extent to include a copy of liability release to go along with the medical release. Although there have been very few claims concerning youth sailing, it is appropriate to discuss this with your attorney if it concerns you.

There should be an adult available on the premises of the program with the emergency numbers of the local hospital and paramedic units. It is also important that numbers for medical helicopter service and the Coast Guard are also quickly within reach, especially if sailors are sailing far away from the actual clubhouse facility.

When at all possible, a program manager should be

on the premises and available to quickly administer these emergency procedures when needed.

In earthquake regions, such as in California, an earthquake preparedness program including emergency supplies, should be available and personnel should be trained to implement the procedures. This may mean that adults near the program should be available to act in assistance when necessary.

An Organized Plan Of Curriculum:

Communication—Home:
1. Is there a calendar of events planned far enough ahead so that there will be no surprises for either you or the staff?
2. Are there bulletins coming home telling you the parent what plans are expected during the upcoming week?

Communication—Between Staff:
1. Do the instructors know what they are supposed to be doing each day?
2. Are there staff meetings planned throughout the week where staff discuss plans for the future? Do any of these include parents? They do not have to, but sometimes it is nice for parents to discuss children's needs with the staff in such meetings.

Daily activity Planned:
1. Are there a variety of activities to keep even the most hard to please youngster interested? Is there a mixture of racing, fun, and social events planned throughout the program? Are there rainy day activities?
2. Is there too much down time for your child so that they get bored or is there too much active time so that they may get too tired?

Discipline Standards:

Does the program have a specific and enforceable discipline standard? It is recommended in most programs that a code of standards be signed by both child and parent before engaging in the program activities. If a child does not adhere to this code of standards, then it is appropriate to call the parent and send the child home. Parents must understand that a program such as sailing, cannot accommodate children who become difficult to manage in a group. Because of safety concerns, it is important to maintain a level of cooperation

Staff Sensitivity:

1. It is assumed that the instruction staff is well trained, but do they understand about child development such as how children learn and play?
2. Is the staff capable of talking directly to each child?
3. Can the staff discuss the child with the parent?
4. Are there problems in *staff conduct* that the child might discuss frequently? Take some of this seriously and talk with the Program Director or Head Instructor. Do not let things "just go away" because they really never do! Sometimes children may exaggerate situations when they are having difficulty adjusting to the program standards and requirements, but sometimes these concerns turn out to be quite real and they should be worked on. Take a moment each day to ask your child how their day went. Listen to both what they say and how they say it! Sometimes their words are not as important as their overall facial and body expressions.
5. Parents must recognize that most sailing instructors are relatively young and are not professional teachers, however, instructors should always act professionally. Instructors will make some mistakes

and they should be reprimanded for them, but all staff should be respectful of parents as well as the children they are teaching. If problems are suspected, contact the Head Instructor or the Program Director to discuss them.

Zero Tolerance For Drugs And Alcohol:

Alcohol and drug use should never be tolerated anywhere or at anytime children are present. In addition, the instructors should never tolerate your child's use of such substances. Be aware that there are some (although not many) programs where such drug use is common, and parents should be quite concerned! I recommend that parents thoroughly check out all programs regardless of the alleged reputation.

A well trained staff makes a major difference in program quality.

Chapter Three
Vocabulary

Aboard- On or within a boat.

A-C Fleet- Sailors are traditionally grouped into skill level fleets with C fleet for beginners, B Fleet for intermediate and A Fleet for the most experienced sailors. Usually the competitors themselves know what fleet they are best suited to sail, but written and even unwritten rules governing certain classes of boats may put some limitations on how long a person might be able to sail in a lower skill fleet. For example, in Sabots (Naples version), sailors move into the most advanced Sabot A fleet when they win both a one day regatta and a two day regatta where there are more than eight or more other competitors from at least two different clubs. In the Laser class, a competitor moves into the A Fleet after winning two regattas with at least five competitors sailing at the event.

Abeam- At right angles to the centerline of the boat.

Adrift- When a boat is loose or unattached to its mooring or dock.

Bailer- A container used to remove water from a boat. This is required equipment aboard most small dinghy boats such as Sabots This can be made from an old bleach bottle (keeping the cap tightly sealed) with its bottom cut out. On Lasers, the bailer is inserted and attached to the bottom of the boat and automatically bails the boat out when it fills with water.

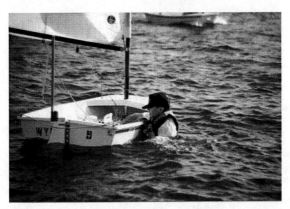

After a capsize a young sailor learns how to bail his boat and get back in.

Ballast- Weight which has been placed in the lower part of a boat to give it stability.

Batten- The thin wooden or fiberglass slats used for sail support when inserted into sewn pockets (Batten Pockets) on the edge of the sail (usually the main). **See Sail Parts**.

Beam- The width of a boat at its widest part.

Beam Reach- The point of sail with the apparent wind coming at right angles to the boat.

Beating- Sailing as close to the wind as possible. **Same as Close Hauled or By The Wind**.

Becalmed- No wind at all. This is one of the most uncomfortable conditions to sail in and takes extreme concentration.

Before The Wind- Sailing in the same direction as the wind. The wind fills the sails from behind. Same as Running.

Bitter End- The last part of a rope or chain.

Block- The official nautical term for a pulley. The metal or wooden shell (**cheek**) acts as a housing for one or more grooved wheels (**sheave**) which acts as a pulley. Two blocks with a line through them forms what is known as a **tackle**.

Boom- The horizontal spar which supports the sail by holding the sail foot.

Boomvang- A wire or line running from the boom to or near the bottom of the mast which holds the boom. This serves to lower the risk of an accidental jibe and helps provide better sail shape when sailing off the wind.

Bow- The forward part of a boat.

Bow Line- The docking line on the front of a boat. Called a painter on most dinghies.

Breakwater- A manmade structure used to break the force of waves at the mouth of a harbor. Races sailed outside the breakwater are considered open ocean races and will be more challenging with waves and current than those races inside the breakwater.

Broad Reach- Sailing with the apparent wind coming over either quarter of the boat.

Bullets- A racing slang term used for first place in a race.

Buoy- A floating aid used for navigation and is also used for sailboat rounding during races.

Burgee- Each yacht club has a unique emblem displayed on a flag known as a burgee. When sailing for a yacht club you sail under their Burgee. People like to collect these from clubs where they sail.

By The Lee- Sailing with the wind behind the boat but blowing from the **leeward** side (the same side where the boom is) of the sail. This can cause the boom to fly over uncontrollably to the other side of the boat, an action called an **accidental jibe**.

By The Wind- Sailing close hauled or beating. **See Close Hauled or Beating**.

Capsize (Turn Turtle)- To turn over in your boat (it happens to all dinghy sailors). Turning turtle is when the boat is completely upside down in the water. Sailors of small boats quickly learn how to right their boat and continue to sail.

Cat Boat- Boats with only one sail with the mast set well forward (Sabot, Laser or Sunfish).

Centerboard- A blade projecting through the bottom of the hull in the center of the boat which pivots up and down into the centerboard trunk of the boat. It is used to keep the boat from sliding sideways in the water in the same way a daggerboard or leeboard does.

Chute- A slang term for the spinnaker sail.

Class- similar boats which are grouped together such as the Optimist, Sabot, Laser, or Sunfish boats. Class boats are maintained with specific building requirements known as one-design class rules so that all boats of a class are as identical as possible. To avoid unnecessary surprises, make sure you know about all the rules of your particular class before competing.

Cleat- The fitting on which a line can be secured.

Clew- The outermost, lower corner of the sail. **See Sail parts**.

Clew Tie Down- Lasers and certain other classes have a line which goes through the grommet (reinforced hole in a sail) on the clew and around the boom.

Clevis Pin- A pin used to close the U in a **shackle** (U Shaped connector to permanently or temporarily connect things) or to connect to a **turnbuckle** (a fitting used to adjust tension on standing rigging).

Committee Boat- The boat from which a race is conducted.

Come About- Steering the boat so that the bow comes through the eye of the wind and the boat moves from one tack to the other. Steering the other way creates a **jibe**. **See jibe**.

Course Chart- A piece of paper handed out at a race which tells which buoys or marks boats should go around. Each course chart contains several courses from which the race committee may chose to send the racers. Skippers should become familiar with these courses prior to actually racing. The chart should be pasted to the inside of the boat using duct tape and a water proof bag so that it can be referred to throughout the race.

Cotter Pin- A small pin slipped through the end of a clevis pin to secure it and keep it from sliding. **See Clevis Pin**.

Cunningham- A line near the gooseneck on the mast used to adjust the tension of the luff of the sail.

Daggerboard (Dagger Board)- Similar to a centerboard serving the same purpose. Unlike a centerboard, it is removable slides up and down instead of pivoting up and down. It is used in Optimist, U.S. Sabot, and Laser boats among many.

DNF- In sailboat racing this means that a boat did not officially finish the race and is therefore not counted as a finishing boat even if the skipper has sailed the entire course. This may happen as a result of equipment breakdown, lack of wind or sailing the wrong course.

DNS- A term in sailboat racing for a boat which does not start a race. A regatta is made up of several separate races, and if for some reason, one of which is not sailed, the skipper will then receive a DNS as the official score for the separate race in that regatta. **Also see OCS**.

Dolly- A special light weight trailer used to transport boats in and around the parking lot or storage yard by pushing or pulling. These are not used for towing, but can be brought in addition to the towing trailer. Dollies are recommended to take when competing in large regattas where there will probably not be enough club dollies for everyone.

Downhaul- A line attached to the tack of the sail which pulls the sail down the mast. **See Sail Parts** and **Boom Vang**.

Dry Suit- A loose fitting one piece outer wear vinyl suit with tight fitting thick vinyl seals around the neck, wrists and ankles used to protect against cold. It does not let any water in at all, and is mandatory wear in places where the water is unusually cold. May be worn all year around in certain regions. **See Chapter 4: Sailing Equipment and Safety**.

Duct Tape- A gray durable water resistant tape which is easy to tear and is indispensable for quick repairs while on and off the water. A must for every gear bag and tool box! **See Chapter 4: Sailing Equipment and Safety**.

Ease Off- To relieve the tension on a line or sail.

Fall Off- To turn the bow of the boat away from the wind.

Fair- Used to describe the smoothness of a boat's hull. The more fair the boat, the faster it is. Skippers will often sand their boards and the boat bottom using wet-dry sand paper to remove any bumps.

Flying Junior- A popular doublehanded two person boat used in scholastic sailing and junior programs. Sometimes this boat is called an FJ or CFJ.

Foot- The lower edge of the sail. **See Sail Parts**.

Foul Weather Gear- Protective outerwear used to prevent the sailor from getting too cold. One piece suits are good for junior sailing when the sailor is not expecting to capsize. Dry Suits are used to keep all water out even when the sailor is in very cold conditions. Wet Suits are tight fitting rubber suits (either short or full length) which let in a thin layer of water which warms when close to the skin surface and is used when sailors are frequently in the water. Ask the program director what conditions are like in the region you are sailing. Experienced sailors will quickly steer you in the right direction. **See Chapter 4: Sailing Equipment and Safety**.

Ghosting- Silently sailing in almost no wind. This is especially beautiful at dusk when the waters are still.

Gooseneck- Hinged fitting on the mast which connects the boom to the mast. Should keep an extra one in the toolbox when dinghy sailing.

Grommet- A metal ring in a sail which allows lines to be connected to the sail.

Gudgeon- See Rudder.

Gunwale- The upper edge of a boat's hull or side.

Hail- To call another boat over. The race committee may hail boats to come nearby in order to pass on instructions.

Halyard- See Running Rigging.

Head Up- Turning the boat into the wind. The opposite of **Heading Off**.

Headway- Refers to the forward motion of a boat.

Header- To head off or away from an original intended course because of a wind shift while the boat is sailing close hauled (**beating**).

Headsail- The sail set forward of the main mast. It may be a jib or spinnaker in small boat sailing.

Head Of The Sail- The top corner of the sail. **See Sail Parts**.

Head To Wind- The boat's bow is directly into the wind.

Heel- When the boat lies over at an angle while sailing.

Hiking Boots- Thick vinyl boots which are reinforced along the top designed to assist sailors by strengthening the ankles. Foul weather gear is usually tucked into the boots to create a water tight seal. **See Chapter 4: Sailing Equipment and Safety**.

Hiking Out- The action of stretching the body over the edge of the hull to help keep the boat flat and counteract the heeling while sailing close hauled.

Hiking out helps to flatten the boat against the wind.

Hiking Pants- Specially designed pants with padded leather patches on the back which are used to support a sailors thighs while hiking out. Most commonly used by Laser sailors to give them more strength and endurance and to save money on worn wet suits and shorts. **See Chapter 4: Sailing Equipment and Safety.**

Hiking Strap- A strap placed in the soul or bottom of a dinghy for a sailor's feet to slip under while hiking out.

Hull- The actual body or shell of a boat without the rigging.

Inspection Port- A hole in the hull of a boat, commonly found in Lasers or on the **thwart (center seat)** of Sabots. It is used to allow skippers to reach inside to check fittings (bolts) and to even store gear such as food or light weight jackets. These are handy to include in your boat when possible.

In Irons- When a boat is stalled because it has headed directly into the wind. This is caused as a result of no wind pressure on either side of the sail. The skipper must turn the boat to either side in order to increase speed.

Jib- The forward smaller triangular sail.

Jibe (Gybe)- To turn the boat away from the wind where the **stern (back end)** of the boat passes towards the eye of the wind while running.

Knockdown- When a boat is knocked over (laid over) on its side by the wind or the sea. This usually allows water to flow over the side.

Lay- To lay a mark means that the skipper can reach a specific mark on the tack (direction) the boat is currently on and does not have to change direction before turning around the mark.

Lee- To be on the downwind side. To be in the lee of an object is to be sheltered by it.

Leeboard- Hangs off the side of a boat and pivots up and down (Naples sabots use these) and acts like a dagger-board to prevent side motion.

Leech- The outside edge of the sail. **See Sail Parts.**

Leeward- The side away or opposite from the wind.

Leeway- Sidewise slipping motion of the boat away from the wind caused by the wind.

Lifejacket- (Personal Flotation Device or PFD) Required to be worn properly by all juniors in most programs. The vest type of jacket is acceptable if Coast Guard Approved. **See Chapter 4: Sailing Equipment and Safety.**

Line- A rope on a boat chosen for different functions.

Luff- The forward edge of the sail. **See Sail Parts.**

Luffing- To describe the sail when it is shaking back and forth because the boat it pointed into the wind.

Luff-in- A name given to certain informal regattas in many regions.

Main- The mainsail or largest sail attached to the mast. **See Sail Parts.**

Mainsheet- A line used to control the boom and the mainsail. Each type of boat requires a different length of such line depending upon the length of the boom and size of the mainsail. A little more than 3 times the length of the boat should provide ample length for the mainsheet. Line should be thin enough to fit through all of the blacks easily, yet thick enough to cleat properly.

Marine Tex™- A particular brand of putty used to permanently fill small cracks and holes in boat hulls and boards.

Mast- Vertical spar which supports rigging and sails.

Mast Step- A shaped brace (usually placed into a molded area of the hull) where the bottom of the mast fits. This should be checked periodically since the stresses of sailing may actually weaken the surrounding hull and cause cracking.

Mast Tube- The sewn sleeve in a sail where the mast slides.

Mooring- An arrangement for securing a boat to a mooring buoy or dock.

Oar —A paddle used to row or steer a boat. A ping pong paddle or a purchased small oar may serve this purpose. This is mandatory equipment on certain small boats to help skippers move away from danger when their sails are not powering the vessel.

OCS- On the Course Side is now the official term for starting a race early before the proper signal. This results in the boat being on the starting side of the race prematurely which means that boats have crossed the startline before the sounding horn or gun. Such a start means that the boat will be given a disqualification **(DSQ)** unless the skipper restarts the race according to the official Racing Rules.

Off The Wind- Sailing to leeward or away from the wind. Opposite of **On The Wind**.

One Design- Classes of boats which are built to strict rules assuring that all boats of a class are as similar as possible. Sabots, Optimists, Lasers, and Sunfish, are all one design classes.

Outhaul- An adjustable line or wire used to secure the mainsail to the back of the boom.

Painter- The line attached to the bow of the boat used to secure a vessel. This can sometimes be used as a tow line. This line should be long enough to allow the boat to move away from the dock so other boats can also tie up next to it.

Paint Pen- A permanent marker which marks on any surface is useful to label gear.

Pinch- To sail a little too close to the wind. This will usually stall the sail and slow the boat down.

Pintle- See **Rudder**.

Point Of Sail- The direction a boat is moving in relationship to the wind.

Port- Refers to the left side of the boat. This also refers to the direction a boat is sailing. Port tack means that the wind is coming over the port (left) side of the boat.

Protest- An appeal of a sailing rule infraction. When one sailor thinks that another sailor(s) has violated such a rules, the sailor may appeal by submitting a written protest to a part of the race committee called the **Protest Committee** which will conduct a formal hearing of both parties before issuing a decision. **See Chapter 5: The Race**.

Puff- A gust of wind.

Purchase- A system of leverage used to move an object. To get is to create purchase.

Ratchet Block- A large block in the center of the boat used to better control the mainsheet . These blocks have a clicker on them.

Regatta- A series of races (usually five or more) over one or several days.

Rigging- Refers to the control lines for the sails and support system for the mast of a boat. Sometimes this is separated into standing and running rigging.

Roach- The amount of curve designed into the back of a sail. **See Sail Parts**.

Rudder- A flat blade hung from the transom used for steering. **Pintles (pins)** are inserted into **Gudgeons (eyes)**. Pintles and gudgeons occasionally stick or bend and tools should be made available in the toolbox to help separate these if needed.

Rules Of The Road- Safety regulations which govern the lakes and oceans so that boats can move safely through these waters. Racing rules make use of these rules to establish a safe and competitive sport for all to enjoy. **See Chapter 5: The Race**.

Run- To sail with the wind behind the boat.

Running Rigging- All wires and lines which are hauled on to handle the sails. This includes the Halyard (used to hoist a sail up the mast); a **Sheet** (used to control and tighten or loosen sails depending upon the wind direction; a **Topping lift** (used to support the weight of the boom when the sail is lowered) a **Clew Outhaul** (controls the tension of the foot of the sail; a **Downhaul** (used to tension the luff of the sail).

S Hook- A heavy duty hook used to permanently connect one end of something and easily connect the other end with the top part of the S.

Sailing Instructions- Instructions prepared by the race committee and handed out at each regatta telling the sailor the schedule for the day, the starting order for the race, and any special rules which will be followed for that particular regatta. Most regattas are sailed under the **US SAILING** rules, but amendments will be noted in the sailing instructions. **See Chapter 5: The Race**.

Sail Parts- Sails are used to power the boat and each part of the sail has its own special name. Sail makers work with sail cloth and the design of each section of the sail in an effort to create the fastest sails.

Shackle- U-shaped hook used to permanently or temporarily connect things.

Sheave- The grooved wheel or roller in a block.

Sheets- Ropes (lines) used to specifically control the sails.

Shroud- The standing rigging that supports the mast.

Singlehanded- Sailing alone in the boat. **Doublehanded** refers to sailing with one other person acting as crew. Larger boats may be sailed with more than two crew.

Skippers Meeting- A short meeting scheduled before each regatta where instructions for the day's event will be handed out and discussed. These meetings are sometimes mandatory and some representative (it may be the parent) should be present to receive any information which might be vital to the day's performance. **See Chapter 5: The Race.**

Snapshackle- A hook with a spring loaded safety catch across the end.

Spinnaker- A lightweight, three cornered sail which is used for running (down wind sailing). Often multiple colored and flying like a parachute in front of the boat, the spinnaker is controlled by using a pole and sheets from each clew.

Skipper and crew flying their spinnaker (chute)
downwind to the leeward mark.

Sponge- Recommended equipment on some boats to mop up water which can make the boat very slippery and uncomfortable while sailing.

Spreaders- Horizontal struts attached to the upper part of the mast to help increase the strength of the shrouds which hold up the mast.

Spring Clip- Used to secure the rudder in place and keep it from floating upward. The spring clip is pressed in to remove the rudder.

Standing Rigging- All rigging and hardware which is used to support the mast and keep it upright and straight. Standing rigging ncludes **Shrouds** (supports the mast from side to side) and **Backstay** (supporting the mast in the back to prevent forward movement)) and **Forestay** (supporting the mast in the front to prevent backward movement).

Starboard- Refers to the right side of the boat. It also refers to the direction **(tack)** the boat is sailing when the wind is coming over the right side **(starboard)** of the boat.

Stay- The part of the standing rigging that supports the mast in the front (bow) and back (stern) of the boat.

Stern- The back of the boat.

Step- The socket where the mast bottom fits. To "step the mast" means that the mast is put into place on the boat.

Stow- To put things away.

Swamp- To accidentally fill the boat with water as a result of tipping the boat too far to one side.

Tack- Refers to the changing direction of the boat when the bow passes through the eye of the wind. **See Port and Starboard**.

Tack- The lower front corner of the sail.

Tangs- Metal strips used to connect the boom to the gooseneck.

Tiller- The handle by which the rudder is controlled.

Tiller Extension- A hinged extension of the tiller which allows the skipper to control the rudder from a distance while hiking out or sitting forward in the boat. These are pre-made and can be purchased for each type of boat sailed.

Towline- A line which is thrown to a competitor from a chase boat or committee boat and is used to tow the sailor to or from the venue.

Transom- The flat part of the back of the boat.

Trapeze- A support used by the crew to enable them to hike far out and away from the actual hull and to gain extra weight to counterbalance the heeling motion of the boat.

Traveler- A rope, rod or track running across the boat on which the block carrying the sheet slides back and forth.

Trunk- The part of the boat that houses the centerboard.

Windward- Moving towards the wind. **Opposite of Leeward.**

Wake- The visible trail of water off the stern of the boat. Wakes from other boats might cause turbulence and may be a cause of capsizing.

Waterline- The painted line on a hull used to indicate the proper balance and trim of a boat. The waterline should be somewhat even when a boat is well balanced.

Whisker Pole- A spar used to extend the jib while running.

For an excellent reference book on sailing vocabulary, look for the book:
   Sailing as a Second Language: An Illustrated Dictionary by Fred Edwards, International Marine Publishing Company, 1988.

CHAPTER FOUR
SAILING EQUIPMENT
AND SAFETY

In sailing, equipment becomes important both for its durability and its safety. This chapter will discuss the types of boats most frequently sailed as well as some of the equipment needs for the junior sailor. In addition, I have included a discussion of important traveling tips for the competitive regatta sailor. Performance and safety are dependent upon the condition of the equipment which is used. Parents should frequently check with their child about any broken parts or pieces which need to be replaced. The child's entire sailing experience will be so much better if everything works as it is supposed to.

The Boat:

To begin with, active junior and community sailing programs will have already chosen a particular boat to sail based on a certain set of criteria and then ask students to either bring their own such boat to the program, or else charter or borrow a boat directly from the program. If purchasing your own boat, expect the prices to vary from $200 to $3500 depending upon the class and newness of the boat. I recommend asking the Program Director if any boats are available on the used market or if boats are provided in the program for the beginning sailor. For example, Westlake Yacht Club offers both options to the sailor with a discount given to those who bring their own boats. At Del Rey Yacht Club and California Yacht Club, kids are asked to bring their own U.S. Sabots and Lasers while the double-handed CFJs and 420s boats are provided free as part of the program. At King Harbor Yacht Club, the junior program uses equipment which has been purchased by a special Youth Foundation, but there are restrictions on when that equipment can be used. It is best to check with various yacht clubs in the harbor regarding boat acquisition. Club bulletin boards and harbor local newspapers are both great sources to check for boats. However, be prepared to call immediately if you see something interesting.

As discussed in Chapter 1, beginning sailing classes use a simpler boat which is less physically demanding, while more advanced training is con-ducted on sophisitcated vessels which require working with two or more sails. Training boats are usually chosen for their lightweight and simple rigging. These boats usually have extra safety features such as foam-core rudders and hulls which remain floating when capsized. They are also easy to repair and capable of taking a fair amount of abuse from the beginning sailor as he/she develops the necessary skills to advance to the more advanced boats.

Training boats:
The most popular training boat is *The International Optimist Dinghy*. There are over 300,000 of these easy to rig-easy to sail small boats on the water in more than 50 countries. The class is strong and the one-design sailing rules which govern what you can or cannot do to the boat, are strictly enforced. For more

about this class and its development in the United States, write to:

USODA Headquarters
P.O. Box 150127
Altamonte Springs, FL 32715-0127
or Fax to: (407)774-6440
or go to the web at *http://www.USODA.org.*

As popular as the Optimist is in Europe and other countries of the world, it has not succeeded in winning over every region of the United States and there are several other well established classes of boats which have been developed over the years. This makes it hard to choose a single official entry level boat for the entire country. For example, in Southern California there are two well established and rule run classes of a boat called a *Sabot*: The *Naples Sabot (leeboard)* and the *U.S. Sabot (Daggerboard)*. In addition, there is a third class of Sabot called the *Winward Sabot* which is considered to be a developmental class of boat built independently in garages and without the strict class rules governing the other fleets. Another small training boat is the *El Toros* which is sailed in Northern California and looks like a Sabot. In the southern coastal waters of the United States, many beginning sailors learn to sail on a boat called the *Sunfish*. The *Sunfish* is bigger than an *Optimist* or *Sabot*, but its sail is easier to bring down while on the water making it especially good to sail in areas where unnannounced storm conditions develop quickly. Finally, efforts are being made for the larger and more advanced *Lasers* (discussed in the next paragraph) to be equipped with a smaller rig, called a *radial rig*, which enables the boat to be used as both a beginning and an advanced training boat. The radial rig include a smaller Laser mainsail and mast section which is designed to make the boat easier to sail for smaller and lighter people. The problem with using boats for dual purposes is that they are often too heavy for younger children to move on and off the docks. The smaller and lighter boats discussed above are probably the ones you will see while looking into singlehanded programs.

Advanced boats: Singlehanded
As children grow older, they usually outgrow the smaller singlehanded training boats. In the U.S. Sabot class, kids begin to talk about being too big when they reach 120 lb, yet, they may be still too small for the next size singlehanded boat such as the Laser which demands sailors to weigh 160 lb. or more for optimum performance in competitive fleets. The *radial rig Laser* can be sailed well by sailors 105 lb.-150 lb. Lasers are very popular in most of the country and in college sailing. You can contact the Laser Association at:

> North American Region
> 5205 Beacon Drive
> Austin TX 78734
> email: laserclass@laser.org
> Phone & Fax 512-266-8254

Another boat, The *Europe Dinghy* hit the world by storm about 1996. This boat was developed in Europe to accommodate the medium sized sailor as well as women. The boat is best sailed by people under 170 lb. (120-170lb. is considered the optimum weight) and is presently used as the Singlehanded Women's Olympic boat. Several boat builders (mostly in Europe) have entered this market. Based on the most recent schedule of regattas, The Europe Dinghy is allowing the lighter sailor a chance to train and sail throughout the world in heavy competition which may lead to a shot at the Olympic Team.

In International events there are up to 200 people on the line sailing these beautiful and exciting boats. For more information look at:

http://www.europedinghy.com

The *Byte* is another newer design that is sailed in programs and advanced races throughout North America and Europe. This boat is also for the lighter and middle weight singlehanded sailor between 90-160lb. Designed by Ian Bruce who spent 18 years working with Lasers, this boat has become popular with sailors who want a chance at surviving heavy wind conditions and to still have fun. You can find information about this fast growing class at:

http://www.byteclass.org

The *Sunfish* is also a favorite program boat because of its rigging and simplicity of boat handling, although it is not as exciting to sail as the Laser. Using a unique lateen rig, The Sunfish is very popular in areas where weather changes create situations requiring immediate sail reduction. The Sunfish is one of the only small boats that allow the sail to be dropped while out on the water.

Advanced Boats: Doublehanded

One of the newest boats to make headlines in double-handed sailing is the exciting *29er* patterned after the *Olympic Class 49er*. Making its debut in 1999, this thrilling trapeze rigged "top gun" of youth performance sailing is the fastest boat available for its size. Six boat builders have entered the arena and have helped make the 29er both a national and international success. The boat is both lightweight and built with hi-tech strong material to give the added acceleration necessary for a "peddle to the metal ride". The fully battened sails and asymmetrical spinnaker increases downwind perform-ance as well. This ISAF recognized class is sure to become the standard for youth competitive sailing throughout the world.

The 420 (Club/Collegiate or regular) is another two person boat which has been chosen by several national regatta selection committees and collegiate programs on the East Coast. Typically, the collegiate versions are more reinforced in the hull and come with untapered masts 420s are a popular two person boat on the East Coast, Canada and Europe and can be sailed with or without trapeze and spinnaker. The *Flying Junior (FJ or CFJ)* is similar to the 420 and is sailed extensively on the West Coast and by many of the major Collegiate sailing programs throughout the country. The collegiate version FJ is similar to the 420 in that it is more reinforced and the mast is untapered. The 470 is another doublehanded boat sailed in some programs as well as chosen as one of the boats ailed in the Olympics. This is a more exciting larger cousin of the 420, but is more sensitive to breakdown and hull damage.

Other Boats:

Other boats which may be found in programs include *Larks, C-Scows, Y Flyers, Holders, Tasers, Luders, Fireballs, Techs, Shields*, and *Solings*. If a particular boat has not been mentioned here, I apologize. As you might see, there are almost as many different classes as there are programs.

The *Laser II* is a two person high performance sailboat that requires a high degree of skipper and crew cooperation. Like the 29er, this boat is trapeze rigged and is capable of a great ride both up and down wind. However, the boat has developed a reputation of being quite temperamental and requires constant upkeep and care to remain competitive. Although this boat used to be a standard for youth national competition, it is rarely

seen out on the race course except in various Laser
Midwinter and fleet events.

Program boats are not always the most exciting boats
to sail once the junior sailor has developed advanced
skills. Sometimes harbors will encourage "family
owned" boats to participate in a racing program in order
to encourage both adults and juniors to interact. The
Snipe is one such two person boat which has remained
popular throughout the country as a boat the entire
family can sail. Families will trade off crew and skipper
positions for years in this class making it one of the great
family boats ever. Then there are the three person boats
which clubs use to encourage big boat skills. The
Lightening, Thistle, Shields and Flying Scott are just four
of the many varieties of these open cockpit boats. The
Santana 20, The J-22 and J-24 are but three multiple crew
closed cabin racing boats which are sailed throughout
the country in very large fleets. These boats are trailer-
able but heavy and require dry (out of the water) storage.

*A Laser II being rigged
on the beach during a
championship regatta.*

Fortunately, the major championship regattas will select their competing boats and try to announce these decisions in time for programs to develop an early training plan. Boats vary considerably in rigging and sailing characteristics, and kids need time to practice on a particular type of boat. Many of the major regattas will provide the boats and even time to practice for a day or two prior to the actual regatta . It is important to read all announcements carefully and keep in touch with the championships by looking at the official **US SAILING** website or reading *Sailing World Magazine*.

Depending upon where the boat is stored, the removable equipment from the boat should be secured each night. This means that the tiller, centerboard, lines, sail, clips, blocks, or anything else removable, should be put into some protective bag and either brought home or locked away to protect against theft. Even the mast and sails should be secured.

Personal Equipment:
Besides the boat and its equipment, every junior sailor should maintain a bag of extra personal stuff which should be brought to the program each day. This includes:
- A change of clothes including a bathing suit
- Bucket and sponge for cleaning and bailing
- Extra line to use as tie down or replacement
- Extra parts for the boat which frequently might break (ask the instructors of your program for a list)
- Foot wear (waterproof Aquasocks™ or similar type)
- Hat (baseball type is just fine)
- Knee pads (get at a hardware or paint store to protect knees)
- Latest version of the **US SAILING** Racing Rules
- Paddle (for smaller dinghy boats this is usually mandatory)

- Paper and pencil for notes
- Spending money
- Sunglasses (to protect the eyes against sun damage)
- Sunscreen (SPF 15 or higher)
- Towel
- Water bottle
- Whistle
- Duct Tape

A Coast Guard approved *life jacket* is mandatory equipment for most programs. The most common and comfortable such jacket is the vest type jacket made by Omega™ or Extrasport™ or other similar manufacturer. These jackets zip in the front and should be worn at all times while on the water even if a wet suit is also worn. Besides saving one's life in case of an accidental injury, the added buoyancy is quite helpful when trying to get back into a capsized boat. Your sailor might not wear the jacket if it is not comfortable, so make sure that the jacket is easy to get on and off and is not overly confining. There is a new line of inflatable life jackets that are being used on the race course, but these are quite expensive and are not really necessary for junior dinghy sailing. Every few years there are changes in design of life jackets, so I recommend that parents should ask around the local marina for what is considered "cool" and safe and comfortable. If other kids are wearing the same type of jacket, you can be sure that your young sailor will also.

Specialty Equipment:

For Laser, Europe or Byte sailors, *hiking pants* are seriously recommended for both comfort and clothing protection. These are specially designed pants with padded leather patches on the back. The pants are used to support a sailor's thighs while they are hiking out while going upwind. These pants are used to give added strength and endurance to the sailor as they sail in heavy air. In addition, the pants save money on worn wet suits and shorts which are always ripped apart in just a few wearings by the rough deck.

In addition to the above equipment, there are some specialized clothing requirements for sailing in cold weather or water. Since *Hypothermia* (a critical lowering of body temperature) is a serious health hazard when exposure to unusual cold occurs, all sailors should remember to protect against such conditions. Dressing in layers is recommended for increased warmth and flexibility. Although only bathing suits are worn under wet suits, warmer clothing can be worn under spray suits, windbreakers and dry suits. Socks should be worn under sailing boots to help protect the feet from cold and blistering as well as to aid in removal of the boots. See the glossary of terms in **Chapter 3: Vocabulary** for further explanation of these personal safety suggestions.

A *wet suit*- This rubber suit should be worn if capsizing for long periods of time are expected. Laser sailors often wear this protective clothing.

Spray suit- Lighter than a wet suit, this clothing may come in one or two pieces and be worn over existing clothing for warmth and protection against spray. It should not be worn if the sailor is going to get very wet since the suit is not water tight.

A *dry suit*- Does not allow any water in and can be used in especially cold water areas such as on the East Coast during winter or the Great Lakes most of the summer. This suit is quite expensive, but is necessary for full outer protection in adverse conditions.

Sailing gloves- made by several manufacturers, these leather gloves protect hands against blistering and wear when grabbing lines. Recommended for anyone sailing

Sunfish, Lasers, or any smaller boat for long periods of time or in heavy wind.

Sailing boots- All young sailors should wear protective waterproof footwear such as Aquaboots to protect against stubs, bruises and cuts. For advanced Laser sailing, high top rubber boots made by Douglas Gill™ or West Marine™ (or any similar manufacturer) is recommended to add strength to the ankles and help with hiking.

Hat over ears- In very cold climates, it is recommended that a lined hat with ear protectors be worn even in summer if the conditions warrant such clothing.

Travel Toolbox:
For the traveling regatta sailor, a complete toolbox should be developed and transported for every race. The following suggestions are adapted from an article by Brian Weeks which was reprinted in *American Sailor Magazine* (Dec. 1992). Although it appears from this list that you may be expected to bring your entire house and garage, most of these items are small enough to fit comfortably into a plastic toolbox (tackle box). Our family has been caught without some of these items in the past, and the results can be disastrous. Think ahead and your racer will benefit.

- A small tack hammer for quick release of stuck rudder pintles or hammering pins back into place.
- Phillips screw driver (medium sized)
- Pliers
- Medium regular screw driver
- Adjustable wrench (medium)
- A putty knife
- 1" chisel
- Two Box wrenches. Check your boat for the standard size you need.
- A battery operated drill and all its bits
- Tube of silicon to fix bailer or other fitting leaks.

- Sandpaper for repairs and fairing the bottom hull and boards. Use wet-dry 600 paper for this work
- Marine Tex™ or Bondo™ works for repairs
- Small plastic boxes for storage
- West System™ repair pack and small amount of fiberglass cloth.
- Black electric tape
- Duct Tape
- Extra assorted lines for quick repair
- Spare bolts and screws and washers for rudder and gooseneck
- Extra cleats and blocks and stern plug (if needed)
- Pop Rivet™ gun for quick repair of mast parts
- Swiss Army Knife™ or general rigging knife
- Matches or cigarette lighter for burning the ends of line

Finally, when traveling, boats may be transported by using a trailer or the roof of a car (called car topping). If you decide to car top the boat, carefully secure all tie downs. Do not use stretchable line, and stop often to recheck for loose ties. Many of us who have traveled have watched with horror as a boat flies from the car onto the highway. Trailers make it easier to transport some of the larger boats. These trailers may be home made with wooden storage boxes built into the structure to accommodate boards, line and sails. There are some very creative trailers at every regatta. But again, make sure the tie downs are securer and the electrical connections are working in the hitch assembly. Also, make sure that your car and hitch are strong enough to tow both the boat and the trailer. Caution, read your motor vehicle code and drive in the slowest two lanes to avoid any unwanted tickets!

CHAPTER FIVE
THE RACE
BY PAUL ARTOF

So, now that Johnny knows something about how to find the wind and keep his boat moving in a forward direction, he might decide it is time to enter his first race. He tells you that he is to be at the water's edge on Saturday morning at 9:30 AM. You ask him what he needs and he shrugs. You ask him how long it will take, and he doesn't know. You ask him whether you should stay at the race site, and he turns on the television. So, what are you supposed to do? You don't even know if you should pack a lunch for him or give him spending money. And, what about medical help if he hurts himself? Does anyone know anything? Well, let's see if we can eliminate some of this confusion.

The Race Day:
Like the script of a play, every race has a pattern of events that take place. The following maps out this sequence.

Preparation:
A parent is the first level in the organization of the young sailor. When my son began to compete, it became important to plan ahead and make sure that appropriate clothing and boat parts were brought to the race course. Although we tried to encourage our young sailor to be

personally responsible, it was important for us to be a major part of the planning. Parents may help in the preparation phase of race day by making sure to bring most of the following items. If your region or yacht club organizers require more specific things to bring, include those as well. (**See Chapter 4** for a more complete list):

1. Change of clothing
2. Life jacket
3. Sailing gloves
4. Stern Plug (for certain boats)—somehow they are frequently missing when we get to the boat
5. Extra line and maybe that old roll of duct tape
6. Lunch, snacks and lots of water —if they will be offshore for a long period of time
7. Some extra spending money so they might buy a drink or candy bar or make a phone call

Rules:
Although it may not look like it from the water, there are specific rules that govern a sailboat race. It often amazes me that most children were able to learn them and grasp their meaning during the first few years of sailing classes because the parents on the dock certainly had trouble.

US SAILING publishes the first and most basic level of rules and guidelines. These rules are compiled by the *International Sailing Federation (ISAF)* and are adopted by the *United States Sailing Association*. These rules cover almost everything and certainly are well worth being familiar with. A copy of these rules can be obtained from **US SAILING** whose address is located in **Chapter 10** of this book. While you are at it, if you join this association, a complimentary copy of these rules comes along with your membership. Also see **Racing Rules** below.

Assuming that your young sailor has had prior sailing experience, it is worthwhile to review these sailing instructions and rules as part of the race day preparation. Such advanced review has two advantages. The most obvious is that even if you are not fully familiar with these rules, and your child cannot explain one or more of the notations on the sailing instructions, you can encourage him/her to ask for help. This accomplishes the second benefit. You are now in a position to learn more yourself as your proud junior sailor comes back and explains the rules to you.

Events for young sailors are typically held in *one-design* boats. This means that all the boats racing in a certain fleet are all the same. Behind each type of one-design boat, is an Association that makes rules governing the way that particular boat is built, rigged and sailed. It is essential for optimum success to obtain a copy of these unique rules before entering any one-design race. I have seen many good natured and willing parents help their children repair or rig a boat such as a Laser or FJ only to be disappointed by a competitor who protests (see **Protest** below) the race results due to specific one-design rule noncompliance. This protest may be as simple as using a banned manufacturer of a block or putting the sail numbers in the wrong place on a sail. Some class boats are more rigid in their interpretation of the rules than others and everyone should be encouraged to know about these rules.

For many races, the Race Committee will write out additional rules that augment the official **US SAILING** rules. These are called *Sailing Instructions*. The committee may wish to add to, modify or eliminate some of the rules that are provided by **US SAILING** or the one-design class. If there is a conflict, these sailing instructions override any conflicting **US SAILING** rules. These instructions are likely to be unique to a particular Yacht Club, location or racing event and it is important to be sure to review these with your young sailor before each race.

Just prior to the race day, the race committee will gather all of the competitors into one area to give last minute instructions or to make last minute changes in the Sailing Instructions. This is typically called the *Skippers Meeting*. You are encouraged to attend. This is the last time that the sailors can discuss the race with the race committee. Consequently, a good time to ask questions. Any changes at this time supersede any earlier rules or instructions. Lastly, be sure to check with the race Notice Board. Be sure to ask of its location if you are unsure where it is. This Board is where official notices to skippers reside. These notices could be important.

Hundreds of lasers being rigged on land at CORK in Canada

Race Course:
At the time of the Skippers Meeting, all competitors will receive instructions and a *Race Chart* indicating what the race course will look like and where it is located *(the venue)*. Often, transportation to this site is provided by the race committee with the use of a long rope *(towline)* pulled behind a small power boat. The towline should be tied to the foot of the mast. The mast can better handle the stresses of being towed than the other fittings on the boat.

Competitors will sail their boats up to this towline, grab on to it, and then get a free ride out to the start line. Except for the first time, when some kids are confused by the procedure and may actually fall out of their boats (the towboats always stop and help when this happens), most sailors enjoy this part of the race day. Of course, if the race is sailed nearby the clubhouse or dock, the sailors will sail directly to the venue. The race course is defined by three or more strategically placed marks or buoys. Based on the location of the starting line, one mark will represents a course for sailing up wind *(The Beating Leg)*, one course sailing downwind *(The Running Leg)*, and a course sailed more perpendicular to the wind *(The Reaching Leg)*. Some possible race course patterns are shown below:

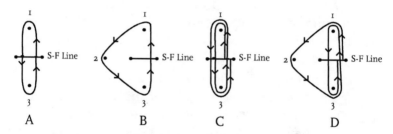

All courses begin at the Start - Finish line (S - F). Possible courses could be:

A. Start, 1, 3, Finish
B. Start, 1, 2, 3, Finish
C. Start, 1, 3, 1, 3, Finish
D. Start, 1, 2, 3, 1, 3, Finish

There are a couple of augmentations that could be added to the above course selections.

1. *Twice Around*: Sail the prescribed A, B, C, or D course twice usually beginning the second rounding by sailing through the Start - Finish line. The race committee would select this option in the event that the wind

velocity was adequate strong. This option would lengthen the race.

2. *Reverse*: Conducted by sailing the above selection of courses by reverse sequence. That is, by beginning the race by sailing mark 3 first. This course would be conducted if the wind were to reverse direction.

The Beginning of the Race:
After all of the boats have arrived at the start line, the Race Committee checks to see that all boats are accounted for. *It is very important to inform the race committee if your child will not be at the start line regardless of the reason.* This could be because of an injury to the skipper or malfunction of the boat. If the committee is unaware of the situation, it could delay the start of the race or cause a search to begin. In this case safety boats may be deployed to look for missing sailors instead of looking out after those on the water.

The sounding of a *horn blast (or whistle)* and the raising of a *class flag* begins the starting sequence of the race. This flag could be an alpha or numeric code flag or a flag that has the sailboats class logo. The shape and design may have been covered in the skippers meeting earlier. There is usually one minute before a *Preparatory or "P" flag* is raised and then three minutes before it is lowered. One minute later the Preparatory flag is lowered (total of five minutes) and the race begins. The raising of the first flag is a way that the Race Committee announces a warning that the race will begin soon. One minute later, the "P" flag announces to be prepared *(on your mark)* and after three more minutes the lowered "P" flag announces *(get set)*. Finally, The lowered class flag announced the start *(go)*. This entire sequence between the raising of the "Class Flag" and its being lowered takes 5 minutes. Some yacht clubs condense this process by having each flag listed above, but reducing the interval between flag movements to one minute each. In this case the sequence is 3 minutes.

The Race Begins:

It is so hard to be a parent and watch your child in one of their first races. All of that commotion out there with boats going everywhere and there is your child sailing his/her boat with sails flapping helplessly, behind a bunch of other boats which are sailing sharply upwind. What happened? What happened is not nearly as important as what you do about it. Many parents inadvertently fully humiliate their child by shouting out advice or criticism. It is probably best to remain silent until your young sailor returns to the dock. At that time, be cool and ask how it went. It is amusing but painful watching non-sailing parents confronting their sailing children and trying to offer advise. If you fit this classification, it is best to ask the sailing instructor to interact on your behalf. This accomplishes two things. 1) The child will take the advice more seriously without straining the relationship with you and; 2) You may be incorrect in your observation and remedy which may only confuse your young sailor. Worse, you may precipitate an argument between you and your child or you and other parents on the dock! Now that's humiliation.

At the start it is close racing which requires concentration, flexibility and courage.

Race Rules (Rules of the Road):
At this point, I will cover just a few rules that might help you to understand the complicated nature of a sailboat race. There are a lot of racing rules set forth by the *International Sailing Federation (ISAF)* and made available by **US SAILING**. Some of the rules change after four years and every sailboat racer should have the most recent rule book.

Right of Way:
1. A port-tack yacht shall keep clear of a starboard tack boat.
2. When on the same tack or jibe, a boat upwind will keep out of the way of a boat downwind.
3. When on the same tack, A boat behind will keep out of the way of a boat ahead.
4. When coming from behind and passing on the downwind side of a boat that is ahead, the boat passing will initially allow the other boat an opportunity to stay out of its way.

Protest:
The above mentioned rules are just a fraction of the plethora of rules your young sailor has learned or will eventually learn while sailing in an organized program. There is no shortage of ways to break the rules. As you will notice in sailing, there is no umpire. There is no one individual who makes sure that the game is played fairly. In place of an authority figure, sailing makes use of peer surveillance, a system that usually works quite well.

We stress to our children the concept of right and wrong. We are proud of them when they do the right thing on their own. It brings both of you honor. Consider being in the heat of competition and accidentally breaking one of those many rules. You are in first or second place; will

you still be honorable and disqualify yourself? Hopefully
the answer is yes and sailing competition is based upon
this type of honor. But, to prevent against the possibility
that such infractions are not reported, the official sailing
rules have a built in law enforcement system. When
Johnny breaks a rule and does not disqualify himself or
accept an alternative penalty, Ernie can immediately indicate to Johnny (using official procedure as described in
the rules) that he saw the incident and will report him.
Ernie initiates this action by telling the Johnny that he is
"*Protesting*" him. If he doesn't know Johnny personally, or
if in the heat of competition, he cannot make out who the
skipper is, Ernie can possibly identifying him by the
number on Johnny's sail. Once this happens, Johnny
must accept or deny his responsibility. This is a measure
of Johnny's sportsmanship. All of this takes place immediately after the infringement. Let us suppose that Johnny
accepts the guilt.

If an *alternative penalty* is provided for in the sailing
instructions, then you will probably see Johnny sailing
two continuous 360 degree turns *(called a 720)*. This is
usually the penalty for breaking a sailing rule although in
some races, the penalty may only be one such turn *(360)*
or no alternative penalty is allowed at all. The race committee will have decided upon the nature of their penalty
system prior to the race and it will be noted in the Sailing
Instructions or they will discuss this at the skipper's
meeting. Your son or daughter must check the sailing
instructions and listen carefully in the skippers meeting
to determine what the operating penalty system is. It's
too late once the race has started.

If Johnny does not think that he broke any of the
sailing rules, then he will continue on as if nothing happened. Once Ernie has completed the race, he will sail up
to the Race Committee boat and tell them of the protest

and whom it is against. The skipper of the protesting boat must describe the incident on a *"protest form"* that will be supplied by the Race Committee. They will then convene a Protest Hearing at the conclusion of the regatta. Each skipper is given an opportunity to tell their side of the story and have witnesses appear with their viewpoint. The Protest Committee will allow or disallow the Protest once all of the evidence is heard. Johnny will be allowed to count his score in the race in question if found not to have broken the rules. On the other hand, if found guilty of the infringement, he will then be disqualified and given last place for that race.

Racing is a sport of honor. It prepares your child to be a citizen in the adult world. A word of caution to parents regarding protests. It is alright for parents to listen and support their children in this process for most races, but, there are other levels of championship regattas where parents must not be anywhere near their child immediately after the race. Most race committee protest hearings will discourage active involvement by the parent during the hearing, and it is important to help your child learn the protest procedure so that they are comfortable in the hearing room as either a witness or defendant. Although not always welcomed, protests happen to just about everyone at some time.

Since there are rarely umpires on the race course, protesting helps to keep the sport honest.

Scoring

A regatta is usually made up of more than one race. It is most common for the score in each race to be same as the finishing position. This is called the *low point scoring system*. Second place gets two points, third place gets three points and so on. The first place boat receives one point. Adding the points in all of the races gives the final score. The boat with the lowest overall score will win. There are special tie breaker rules that will be used in case of two or more boats receiving identical scores. You may want to ask the race committee before the race begins how they plan to break a tie. This will assure that there are no surprises at the end of the day.

For more information regarding racing, look for the following books:

1. *Paul Elvstrom Explains the Racing Rules of Sailing:2001-2004*—edited by Soren Krause 208 pages, published 2001, INT25.
2. *Advanced Racing Tactics*, Stuart H. Walker, W.W. Norton and Company Inc, 1976.
3. *Championship Tactics*, Gary Jobson, Tom Whidden and Adam Loory, St. Martin's Press, 1990.
4. *Sail Power: The Complete Guide to Sails and Sail Handling*, Wallace Ross, Alfred A. Knopf, 1975.
5. *Sail To Win Series* published by International Marine. (several books written by different authors on the subject of racing and tactics.
6. ***US SAILING*** *International Racing Rules*, Adopted by United States Sailing Association, 2001-2004 rules.
7. *Winning in One-Designs*, Dave Perry, Dodd Meade and Company, 1984.

CHAPTER SIX
WINNING/LOSING AND SPORTSMANSHIP

Show me a good loser in professional sports and I'll show you an idiot.
 Leo Durocher
 Baseball Manager

Defeat is worse than death, because you have to live with defeat.
 Bill Musselman
 Basketball Coach

In 1994, a chilling story of misaligned competitive values electrified readers and viewers alike and still carries an after image today, years later. Olympic figure skating hopeful Nancy Kerrigan was assaulted after her skating practice and was unable to defend her National Figure Skating Championship title, a supposedly necessary step to be named for the 1994 U.S. Olympic Team. Her chief rival, Tonya Harding, skates to victory and secures a berth on the Team. Later, it is revealed that Tonya's bodyguard and husband may have been involved with hiring a hitman to break Kerrigan's knee cap in order to keep her from competing. Arrests are made and a dark shadow is cast over the sport of figure skating.

In interviews with other skaters it is revealed that it is not unusual for skates to be sabotaged, music tapes to be lost or destroyed, or threats to be made just

before a competition. Most of this is done to young children on their way up the competition ladder. It seems
that kids can have crazy parents willing to do almost anything to assure their champion darlings some success.
What might a 23 year old desperate competitor do when
they have lost almost everything else in their lives but
their sport?

In a recent sports broadcast, the sportscaster begins
by reporting a story about uncontrolled fighting on the
basketball courts. This is followed by a discussion of the
usual technical fouls in the hockey rink and a story about
the increased disturbances on the baseball diamond. At
the end of the sports hour, the newscaster shakes his
head and asks an unseen audience, "What ever happened
to just plain old sportsmanship?" A good question to ask
Nancy Kerrigan who continued on her path to the 1994
Olympics despite her injury, but who will never forget her
ordeal, however many championships she skated. Her
life has been altered forever. If we could, we might ask
this question of Leo Durocher, Bill Musselman (see the
quotations at the beginning of this chapter) or any of the
modern day professional coaches who believe in winning
at all cost.

It is obvious that professional sports is becoming
excessively expensive to maintain. It can cost over
$70,000 per year to become an Olympic skater, which is
perhaps the motivation to play hard and play for keeps.
But, should winning override decency? I am afraid that
we are passing this win at all cost message down to our
young athletes even before they have decided to become a
professional athlete. If winning is for winners, and losing
is for jerks, then what about the 99% of the athletes today
who are willing to work hard to excel at their sport with
all that they have to give regardless of the results? Should
they just pack up and go home? And what about the

winner today when he or she loses tomorrow? How will they cope with that? Can a tennis player win every game or a swimmer every race? Do players resort to cheating because they cannot stand going home and living with the pain of their defeat?

Tonya Harding had a great year in 1990 but an inconsistent 1991 and 1992 when she placed fourth (after reporting almost a week late to the Olympic training camp) behind the third place Kerrigan in the Winter Olympics. Then in 1993 her personal life disintegrated and she slid to a disappointing fourth place in the national championship. Going into the 1994 Olympics, she was not considered to be the front runner. Nancy Kerrigan was. Did Tonya Harding have anything else in her life to help give her identity besides her skating? Or, did those who supported her believe that she needed the added protection for her ego or worse, for theirs? The true motive for Kerrigan's assault may never be known, but the results we do know. Physical and mental assaults on competitors hurt everyone in athletics—skaters, skiers and sailors along with hockey players, football players and baseball players—all of us are assaulted when players cheat to win.

Parents are a strong influence in their children's perception of themselves in relationship to others on the playing field. For example, a little league parent who sends the message to their child (even nonverbal) that he/she will only be loved if they win, is really setting the child up for a lifetime of failure. Why? Because that child soon learns that winning at all cost is what matters most. These children perceive that winning is equated with love, and they also learn that a good attitude, self respect, and honor are of little value. Eventually, someone who is younger, faster, or stronger challenges the ability of this performance compulsive competitor, and the result may be to turn that person towards performance enhancing substances or cheating behavior to ensure the win. I've seen kids blatantly cheat in a race and ignore the rules or bully their way past other competitors. When confronted by someone in authority, the child too often replies that "Everyone does it; so why shouldn't I?" Or "I don't see what's wrong with it as long as you don't get caught."

Then there are the kids who feel that they just cannot relax without one more hit on their hand rolled joint or snort of white powder. Great stuff, we're teaching our kids. Let's for a moment, examine how this win at all cost attitude can develop in even the youngest or most talented youth.

Winning, Losing and Self Handicapping:

Is it possible for a winner to set himself up to lose? This is the question Steven Berglas and Roy Baumeister raise in their book *Your Own Worst Enemy: Understanding the Paradox of Self-Defeating Behavior* (Published by Basic Books, 1993). Berglas and Baumeister suggest that it is common for people who are highly successful and perhaps even obsessed with success and winning, to engage in self destructive behavior that assures them an *increased chance to lose*. They call this phenomenon *self handicapping* and it occurs even more when these success oriented people are confronted with increasingly tough competition. In other words, as people become more and more used to winning, they develop an increased fear of losing. As a result, they establish unconscious credible excuses for their loses in order to save face. In Joannie M. Schrof's review of *Your Own Worst Enemy*, in the May 17, 1993 issue of *The U.S. News & World Report*, she suggests that, "It is often success that leads people to flirt with failure." I've seen this type of self handicapping in sailing many times. A champion sailor is late for a regatta because his car runs out of gas. The equipment on a chartered boat breaks down due to a simple malfunction which could have been avoided if it had been checked carefully in the morning. A young sailor about to sail his first advanced fleet race wakes up with a bad stomach ache and cannot compete or just sleeps in too late and cannot get to the start line on time. Each of these excuses effectively keeps the winner from having to really face the competition. How convenient. "I lost because of _____."You can fill in the blanks with anything. The disappointment of the lose is lessened because there is a credible excuse. But, what would have really happened if they had actually raced.

Now, if the competitor is really terrified of matching themselves against the newest threat, then how do they continue to compete? A successful young sailor, who has been raised to believe that they are only as good as their publicity, may take on ever more dangerous handicaps such as drinking or other major drug use in order to relax and loosen up. The danger of this is usually obvious to everyone but the user. If one loses a race while high, and is sloppy at the start or hits a mark during an upwind maneuver, they can pass off the loss to being tired or just not on that day. Their equipment failed them (they were too high to check it); their competitors were stupid; the Race Committee was untrained; the race wasn't important; the party went on too long; who cares about this dumb race anyway. This is the classical pattern of self denial.

Although occasional rationalization (excuse making) is an important part of coping with stressful situations for all of us, the chronic user of self handicapping never learns how to get back into the winner's circle fear free. We have all read about major league baseball stars who fall from grace because of drug use, and we have asked ourselves how a player making $12 million can throw it all away? These players have never really learned how to get back up from defeat, and they choose to run away rather then risk to win. Well, it appears that non-professional players can also throw away their futures because they fear losing more than anything else. To quote one of the parents I used to spend time with on the docks.

"You can't win unless you risk losing."
    Lois Good
    California Yacht Club

I couldn't agree more with this. Even the most talented national champion will one day find someone behind them trying to take away the title. Kids must learn how to take the risk of losing in order to become winners in life.

Sportsmanship:
Sportsmanship: "One who exhibits qualities especially esteemed in those who engage in sports such as fairness and self control."
    (American College Dictionary)
"A person who is fair, generous a good loser and a gracious winner."
    (Webster's 9th New Collegiate Dictionary)

In analyzing the above definition, sportsmanship, is really about developing *self esteem* and *moral behavior*. A child who feels good about him/herself can sail through life as a winner no matter what the win/loss column in the sports page reads. There is no question that winning in a competitive sport feels great —perhaps one of the greatest feelings a young person can experience. But, learning how to conduct themselves as socially graceful people, both on and off the competitive stage, is the key to a lifetime of success. Fairness, graciousness, self control are all part of this conduct.

Can one learn to be a sportsman without losing the competitive spirit? Leo Durocher may not think so, but **US SAILING** sure does and recognizes sportsmanship when it is present. Today, it is quite common for programs and organizations to hand out special sportsmanship awards and incentives during the end of the year trophy presentations. However, I might question whether or not we actually value these awards as much as the first, second or third place winner's trophies. I have heard kids who have won some of these high honors laugh self consciously about them and say that they are not real awards anyway. They feel that they are consolation prizes. How far from the truth can this be. If anything, we should value sportsmanship above any other awards. These sportsmen should be considered our role models. So how do we as parents elevate sportsmanship? We must value it as well.

Self Esteem and Sportsmanship:
Parents may help to develop the value of sportsmanship in their children by increasing both a child's self esteem and moral behavior. Here are some reminders in a list I adapted from the *National PTA* and *March of Dimes Joint Parenting: The Undeveloped Skill Project* several years ago. In lecturing and talking to parents about these reminders, I am always surprised by how many parents just forget that their children are indeed just children.

Eleven Steps To Better Self Esteem:
1. Show respect to your child and allow for individual action within a given limitation.
2. Define and enforce limits and rules and communicate the family value system clearly. Let the child know what is expected of them.
3. Reward each child when possible-verbally as well as

with action. Praise, recognition or special privileges are often good rewards for a good job.

4. Take your child's ideas seriously. Listen to them. They make sense more often then you might think. Don't put the child down just because their ideas seem different from yours. Discuss where they developed their beliefs and why you cannot agree with them. Often, what you may hear gives you clues to their fears and concerns.

5. Have reasonable expectations about what they can or cannot do. Understand that there are age differences in development and punishment should be age appropriate.

6. Help your child to develop tolerance for their own actions and those of others. Help them to understand and accept differences in people and help them appreciate strengths in others as well as themselves.

7. Remind them just how special they are—even if they do not win!

8. Be available for them even if they chose not to take advantage of it all of the time. Being there is still important to them.

9. Tell them you love them regardless of their performance.

10. Give them increasingly more responsibility appropriate to their age.

11. Let them fail in order to let them win.

Moral Behavior and Sportsmanship:
Developing morality in children is also a parent's responsibility. This requires *parental communication (talking), modeling, and reinforcement of appropriate behavior* in what I call the TMR model of morality development: Talking, modeling, and reinforcement all combine to

help children learn acceptable behavior which translates to sportsmanship.

Talking: Talk to your child about moral and ethical issues which matter in society. Include in that discussion issues related to winning and losing.

Children cannot be expected to pick up morality and ethics without having a forum in which they can express their concerns regarding the inconsistencies of life. Moral development progresses from a very concrete and simplistic view of doing the right thing in order to protect oneself from pain and punishment (avoid getting in trouble because I will get punished, to a more abstract and complex understanding of what is right which encompasses the ethical needs of society (I will rescue this person at any cost because life is more important than the event). Children (and sometimes adults) need help in moving through this concrete to abstract thinking and behavior. When adults are available to communicate a higher standard of moral thinking to a child who is thinking at a less developed level, research has clearly shown that profound changes take place in the child and they take on more of the adult actions and thoughts. The more dialog, the more change.

Modeling: Be a role model for your child and demonstrate appropriate moral behavior at home for the child to imitate.

Learning theory has long demonstrated that children model what they see and hear at home. "Monkey see and monkey do" is quite true when looking at parent-child interaction. It is a demonstrated fact that modeling of poor social behavior, even on the television, encourages poor social behavior. Children have come home after only a few days at a new school with new friends, acting entirely different then the week before. A father or mother who is a bad sport in their games, will no doubt convey this way of behavior to their own children. If we worry about TV cartoons or video games doing damage to our children, what do we think our own behavior as parents might do to a child?

Reinforcement: Reinforcement of appropriate morally based behavior will lead to better self control and more advanced emotional development.

Reinforcement is actually defined in psychology as anything that increases the chances of a behavior being repeated. Reinforcement may be either positive or negative. A *positive reinforcement* (such as praise, food, money or privileges) encourages a child to conduct their behavior in order to seek more of that reinforcement. "I like it", "I want it", and "I'll do more to get it"! A *negative reinforcement* is an unpleasant stimulus which is actually quite unattractive to the child and which is avoided if at all possible. It is not punishment, which is painfully inflicted when we do something wrong in order to get us to stop a certain behavior; but rather, a negative reinforcement encourages us to do a desired behavior in order to avoid the unpleasantness surrounding us. For example, ignoring a child who is having a temper tantrum is considered to be a negative reinforcement rather than a punishment. This is because the usual result of ignoring the child, causes him/her to cease the tantrum. Evidently, the lack of social response by the parent is so unpleasant, that the child is actually encouraged to do something to stop the lack of attention...in this case, to stop the tantrum. Negative reinforcement appears to work far better and for a longer period of time than punishment since giving the child any attention at all, including punishment, only rewards the child for their action. A child's poor sportsmanship may be treated with either direct punishment or withholding of team attention by the coach and other teammates.

Most children enjoy pleasing their parents and seek these reinforcements. The overriding principle in reinforcement is **consistency** when and how such reinforcement is to be used. Once a parent creates a priority of expected social and emotional behavior for their child, the parent must maintain some sort of consistent schedule so that the child can really learn what is expected of them. Further, each parent must agree on the type and amount of such reinforcement. This often becomes a problem in separated families where Mom and Dad are struggling for *good parent honors* with their children. Each parent undermines the reinforcement of the other, only adding to the child's ultimate confusion. It is so important that parents realize the impact of the overall message they are giving their children. Like self esteem, moral behavior is not something learned in a textbook or at school on the playground. If we want our children to grow up and be decent human beings, we must work at what we ourselves are demonstrating. It is hard to ask our children to do something that we ourselves cannot model.

Coaches vs Parents:

Parents have begun to hire personal coaches to help their young sailors achieve more on the race course. This is not inherently bad, but sometimes the coach becomes a surrogate parent and he/she begins to alter the child's perception of right and wrong. Many parents express such exquisite emotion to their children when they win, that sometimes that thrill is misinterpreted as love for the child. In these cases, the youngster learns how to manipulate the system to keep their parent's love and they associate loosing with rejection. These kids risk growing up to be adult cheaters. An excellent young sailor may learn from his coach how to make up a story in the protest room rather than face the truth that another competitor had sailed a little better and made fewer mistakes. This sailor chooses cheating over honesty and his coaches might actually agree with him since they are paid to win. A recent true story found a sailor in a high ranked **US Sailing** Championship, who was quite capable of winning on the water most times, looking the protest room jury in the face and lying to them about the details of a protest he had lodged against the race committee. When confronting his competitors later in the day, he apologized for what he was doing, but never admitted that to the jury. At the end of the event, he lost the respect of his fellow competitors even though he carried the trophy home. He had developed such an impregnable attitude towards winning at any cost, that he jeopardized his reputation to achieve his goal of winning. He is now coaching others to do the same.

Coaching is now a regular part of the sport of sailing. Most major and minor programs use coaches at regattas. Young kids look up to their coaches and use them as role models. If a coach pushes a child too far and too quickly or too dishonestly, the results can have devastating long-term effects. Children have been given a wrong message when parents let the coach become the parent.

Parents help the children get ready for the start.

Words Of Caution!

Winning at any cost is a philosophy which should not apply in any sport, but in sailing, the philosophy can be deadly. Recently, it is being reported that more and more often, kids are getting high on drugs in order to relax and win their race. These young sailors actually believe that they can only win while high. Drug use has become a culture among many of these kids, and these kids reinforce each other in this behavior. It is a sorry commentary on our athletic and social system that young athletes are so stressed out playing, that they are experiencing so much pressure inside. I have discussed this with experts on both coasts, and the general feeling is that this is a relatively new phenomenon at the youth level. Besides the fact that there have been some deaths in the sailing world as a result of drugs, several competitors have found their performance beginning to suffer as discussed in the previous section of this chapter of self handicapping. People have been kicked out of regattas, out of school and out of sailing as a result of this behavior. Sailing can be deadly if safety is not always a consideration.

US SAILING makes it quite clear in the race instructions sent to every youth champion competitor that drugs will not be tolerated in any way from the time the regatta begins to the moment it ends. However, all too often, juniors are encouraged to practice on their own without any supervision or coaching away from regatta sites. Football and basketball maintains a code of performance by the coaches. Sailing is a sport usually void of such active supervised coaching.

It is imparitive that parents wake up and begin to take an active interest in this supervision.

  I. Do not be content just letting your child go to regattas without knowing where they will stay, who they will be with, and what adults are involved.

2. Be sure to check out the coaches for their own views and values regarding performance enhancing substances. All is not necessarily what it seems to be. Do not be afraid to ask questions and to discuss with other parents your concerns.

3. Make yourself available to your child as much as possible during regattas. Make sure they have money and food and water and clothing as needed. Be there to listen if they are having doubts about what they are doing.

Sailing is a demanding sport, and it takes a toll on the competitor. Help your child become a responsible athlete by being a responsible parent.

CHAPTER SEVEN
SPORTS PSYCHOLOGY
BY CLAUDIA WAINER, M.A.

Claudia Wainer holds a Masters degree and is clinically trained in psychology and works with young people as a therapist. Claudia has thirteen years experience working in a junior program setting both as a coach and administrator. Claudia is an accomplished one-design skipper and knows first hand how to pull together a successful campaign.

This Article is written specifically for the child from the child's point of view. If possible, let your child read this section and then work with him/her to implement the ideas. Success in sports requires as much conditioning of the mind as the body.

What Is Winning?

Everyone likes to be a winner. However, just to set your site on winning is not enough. Many components must come together in order to give you that winning edge. Without detail and attention given to these areas, you might as well stay ashore.

In this section, I will discuss how to organize your program, identify and set attainable goals, what it means to be mentally prepared, and how to be a Corinthian competitor. We will also explore how to deal with disappointments when a goal is not realized and how to reduce the effects of performance anxiety and burnout. This chapter is dedicated to the courageous junior competitor.

Organization/Eliminate Surprises:
Lack of preparation is the single most influential element that will cause you to end your sailing season prematurely. Organizing your program must begin at the onset of each racing season and is the grass roots of winning. This means that your equipment, regatta schedule, budgeting, goals and expectations, and all other important travel preparation must be planned for well ahead of each regatta. Attention to all of these details will reduce surprises and help to eliminate stress that develops with last minute planning. For example, in traveling to an out of town regatta, it is better to focus mental energy on familiarization of the race course, local conditions, and strategy than it is on getting housing and last minute equipment which could have been done weeks before in anticipation of the race.

Besides planning for the specifics of any one regatta, a long-term assessment of the financial commitment necessary for a sailing campaign is also necessary in order for you to contact various funding sources well ahead of time to request support. If your preliminary program organization and budget can be presented as a package, it should increase your chances of receiving a commitment from your funding source.

Goal Setting:
Set realistic goals in order to maximize your confidence and minimize your disappointment. It may be more important to underestimate these goals and to later reevaluate them after frequent successes than to overstate them and contend with a lowered self-confidence as a

result. Here are some ways to evaluate your personal goals and motivations and maximize your confidence.

1. *Identify the reasons you are involved in your sport and specifically what personal motivation do you have for sailing.* Which of these motivations apply to you?

   A. Do you crave the competition and the thrills and chills which go along with it? *Or*

   B. Do you aspire to national/international recognition? *Or*

   C. Are you motivated by the simplicity of just being outdoors, having the wind in your face and getting a tan at the same time? *Or*

   D. Are you perfectly happy going out to race and wherever the chips fall is all right by you?

   Once your personal goals and motivations have been identified, then plan your sailing around these. If you are moderately competitive, the sailing program most appropriate for you may be quite different from a person who is highly competitive or not competitive at all. Not everyone is motivated by the same thing.

2. *Identify your long-term goal for the season. What is it you ultimately want to achieve this year in this sport?* Do you want to go to the *Youth Championships* in June or the *Sears, Bemis Smythe* in August? Or, are you happy to finish in the top third of your fleet in a year-end local event? Or perhaps, you may want to finish ahead of a certain other competitor in the *Nationals?* In all three of these cases, you want to highlight this goal and put the essence of your season together.

3. *Develop small short-term goals to help build confidence.* Long-term goals are made up of smaller short-term goals that help to build confidence. This confidence is the key ingredient needed in

becoming a successful competitor. Some important confidence building tasks are:

A. Test the limits of your talents by experimenting with tactics or boat handling which you have not tried before. Stretch your skills and your abilities.

B. Practice often to help sharpen your skills. The execution of boat handling may be the difference between rounding the leeward mark in first place or fifteenth.

C. Expand on little successes and give yourself a pat on the back when you execute a maneuver that is successful. Be quick to recognize the strengths of your race and write what you did to get an edge on the competition. Give yourself positive feedback.

D. Overcome your fears. Every competitor must face the fear of losing, however, much of this fear comes from being (or feeling) unprepared. This is called **performance anxiety** and can reduce peformance itself. Plan ahead and work on the plan to help reduce any fear which is the result of this anxiety.

4. *As confidence builds, begin to identify areas of strength that you should continue to grow, and identify areas of weakness that need special focus.* For example, if my roll tacks are not as fast and smooth as they could be, I might ask my coach to drill me more in this area. If my starts are excellent and well timed, I might continue to practice them but will add more starting techniques to my arsenal so that I can begin to integrate them in practice and in races. If I take someone's stern too often and allow them to get to the favored side of the course, then I might work on becoming more aggressive and exercise my lee bow option.

In all of these examples, I have identified strengths to build upon and weaknesses to work on. These are really short-term goals. If these goals are combined, I become a more competent and skilled competitor that will ultimately assist me in attaining my long-term goals in competition.

Mental Preparation:

Wrapped within the experience of competition are many highs and lows. An "off day", an "awesome" day, a mediocre day, or an outright "bad" day can happen to any of you. Lack of mental focus can make these hills and valleys overwhelming and even more distracting to the competitor. Maintaining your intensity and concentration while training and competing is essential in order to execute solid tactics and boat handling. The bandits that threaten your focus are:

1). Distractions on and off the racecourse.

2) Stress that is caused by anxiety or worrying about your performance.

3) Pressure from outside supporters (perceived or real) such as yacht clubs and parents.

The consequence of allowing these bandits to rob your concentration is that they slow your reflexes. The expression "sailing by the seat of your pants," refers to the experience of sailing when you are barely conscious of the decision making process that your brain is making. In close racing, you need to make split second decisions, and if not concentrating 100% on the task at hand, you may miss valuable regatta winning opportunities. Reflexes are subconscious so you must keep airways open between your brain and your body.

The best way to deal with the distraction, stress, and pressure of racing, is to discipline yourself. You must find the **zone** which effectively blocks non-productive thinking. Like a marathon runner who must pace himself physically, a sailor's mind must conserve energy. Do not have thoughts that take you away from your main strategy. Stop thinking about parents who are watching you from the spectator boat; they are proud of you for just being there. Stop thinking about the yacht club who supported your sailing; the members are enjoying the support of your efforts especially since you are out there representing them so competently. Your mind should be focused entirely on the race and your boat handling, and keep those non-productive thoughts away! This is what finding the zone is all about.

Sportsmanship:
Be a gracious and rule abiding competitor. If you find yourself consistently involved in protests, (filed by either you or someone against you) you are not being a good sportsman. If you are the one who is protested in every race, then you are sailing too aggressively and not sailing smart. Even if you just "sneak in there" fairly and cleanly, your competitor may see it differently and you will find yourself in the jury room defending your fancy move. This will eventually lead to distractions in your overall sailing. Protests take a lot of time to present and to be heard. This takes valuable time away from your ability to focus on the task at hand.

A second reason to reduce your protest time is *invisibility*. Being a fast cut-up on the racecourse is like driving a noisy hot pink double decker bus down the road. After a short time, your competitors are going to want to blow that ugly, noisy, distracting bus out of the water. Instead, be a quiet Mercedes and just purr along. Don't draw unnecessary attention to yourself. Big gains can be made smoothly and quietly, and you will be more respected and successful on the race-course as a result of it.

Don't be a sore loser! This is not part of a winning program and is very non-productive. You may believe that rude behavior is intimidating to the competition. The fact is, not only are you disrespectful when you are a sore loser, but you are also disliked. When you are pounding around on the dock telling everyone how much better you are than they are, guess how much mental energy is blowing in the wind? It's better to keep your lips zipped than to say something that will no doubt get you in big trouble. Conversely, if you come up against someone who is a poor sport, walk away...fast. Remember to remain focused and let the pink noisy double decker bus role on somewhere else.

How To Deal With A Legitimate Loss:
What if you have followed the prescription for running an organized program, assessed your skills and set your goals accordingly, and you suffer more than one disappointing finish? How do you keep going out to the racecourse when you apparently are not getting any better? Here are some pointers to keep your program from sinking:

1. Reframe your loss or losses and look at them as lessons to build upon. How you cope and learn from loss is critical to moving productively forward.
2. Reexamine your goals and expectations. If you are consistently performing outside your target, modify your goals so they are more aligned with your talents.
3. Do not let disappointment become self-defeating. Acknowledge to yourself that all athletes go through a slump. Try to keep a positive attitude and fight having negative thoughts about your performance. In place of the word Can't, substitute Will.

4. Don't lose site of your own abilities and accomplishments. Review your strengths and weaknesses and know that it is almost impossible to forget a learned ability.

5. Work on the areas that are giving you specific problems. For example, if your leeward mark roundings are leaving you on the outside of the pack of overlapped boats, review the strategies in approaching and rounding marks in traffic, and try to apply the tactics during practice races.

How To Reduce Anxiety, Stress and Burnout:

Anxiety and Stress:

Mounting pressures concerning your performance, better known as Performance Anxiety, may cause the state of being stressed out. You may feel that you need to do well to reward your yacht club for their support or win your parent's respect. Such mental pressure may produce the following symptoms: irritability, difficulty in concentrating, sweating, nervousness, and loss of appetite. These symptoms can be experienced in varying degrees and combinations. These mind and body reactions will effectively sabotage all that you have worked for and should be eliminated as much as possible.

A competitor may not be totally stress free since pressure always exists in the realm of any competitive game, however, corralling pressures and reducing stress is possible.

1. Recognize the symptoms of stress. You may experience some of these symptoms right before and during many regattas.

2. If feeling stress before a regatta, you can try the following:

A. Sit down quietly and review what you are stressed out about. Are you concerned about your level of practice? Your parents' expectations? Your performance?

B. Review on paper or in your head (with your coach or parent) all of the areas you have appropriately prepared for and are now ready to execute.

C. Reassure yourself that you have done all of the preparation possible and that you are as ready as you can be.

3. If feeling stress during a regatta, you can try the following:

A. Make two columns on a piece of paper. Write down all of your goals and objectives for the race in one column and your strengths in another. Place these in a watertight zip lock and tape it to a part of the boat easy to see.

B. When stress symptoms appear, review this list. You will begin to replace negative thoughts with positive ones and your focus will return.

Burnout:

Remember when we discussed conserving mental energy? Going all out in the beginning of your campaign can lead to the syndrome called **burnout**. You will know when you are suffering from burnout when you begin to feel unmotivated and lazy and your performance on the water becomes sloppy and erratic.

You can recover from burnout by stepping back and reevaluating your goals and expectations. Lack of focus and purpose use up much needed mental energy and too much intensity lifts the pace beyond reasonable limits. Reestablish short-term goals to help win back the psychological edge and appropriate pacing every competitor requires in their arsenal.

In closing, a successful campaigner has done the necessary pre season planning and has set attainable short and long-term goals. Throughout the season, the competitor has reviewed and reassessed his/her own unique strengths and weaknesses and has implemented ways to maximize and minimize these areas. A competent athlete is also a good sport and is respected by peers on and off the water as well as the governing body of the class of boats they sail in. It is more important to win as a good sport as it is to win. Self confidence is such a large part of a competitor's mindset that any negative thinking or self doubt can turn the best boat handler and tactician into a back of the fleet stressed out has been. Every competitor experiences stress, but the most successful learn to deal with it. Staying focused and maintaining a positive mental attitude will go a long way in putting your sailing skills into practice on the racecourse.

CHAPTER EIGHT
FITNESS FOR KIDS
BY CHRIS CAMACHO

Chris Camacho earned a Masters degree in 2002 from University Of San Fransisco in sports and fitness management. He graduated from Chapman University in 1991 with a degree in movement/exercise science with an emphasis in athletic training. He is an ACE certified personal trainer and has worked with clients both in the United States and Japan for more than twelve years. I asked Chris to write this section because of his unique experience with both adults and children who are involved with many types of sports. Whether playing soccer or sailing, an athlete needs to be physically fit and mentally alert.

In this chapter we will discuss the importance of fitness and its relationship to sailing. First, we must clarify that fitness is described as a state which characterizes the degree to which a person is able to function efficiently. Fitness is the balance between being physically healthy and emotionally sound. As parents, we may find it difficult to change lifestyles and health habits as we grow older, so the earlier we educate our children in fitness, the more likely they will carry the experience into their adult years.

When discussing physical fitness, there are three important areas which should be developed: *cardiovascular fitness, body strength, and flexibility.* All three of these are essential to the physical well being of everyone all of the time, but they become even more important when an individual decides to compete in an athletic sport such as sailing.

Cardiovascular Fitness:

Cardiovascular fitness is considered the most important aspect of the three fitness categories, and must become a vital part of any regular fitness program. By participating in regular physical exercise, the individual strengthens the heart which allows it to pump more blood per beat. A stronger heart makes the heart more efficient both during exercise and at rest. In addition, an improved cardiovascular system enables us to utilize oxygen better during such increased physical activity. A trained cardio-vascular system leads to the body's ability to perform more strenuous exercise for a more sustained period of time. This increased duration allows us to work harder and gain in physical strength. Finally, although this may seem to apply more for older people than for children, cardiovascular fitness helps to lower the risk of coronary heart disease such as atherosclerosis, high blood pressure and stroke. Working with young people to develop fitness habits early, will benefit them later in life.

Muscular Strength:

Muscular strength can be defined as the total amount of force which can be exerted by a muscle with a single effort against resistance. By maintaining muscular strength, either through specific sports training or by a general exercise program, the individual can expect to benefit in several ways:

1. They may reduce the risk of serious or mild injury by increasing the body's musculature.

2. Increased musculature should lead to better posture thereby reducing back problems later in life.
3. Increased muscle strength will increase endurance and provide resistance to muscular fatigue.
4. Increased musculature may help increase the immune system's ability to fight off disease.
5. All of this should enhance performance as a result of increased speed, strength and agility.

Flexibility:
The third and last area to develop in fitness is flexibility. Flexibility refers to the ability of a joint to have freedom of movement through its normal range of motion. By maintaining adequate flexibility, the individual will reduce the risk of orthopedic conditions such as low back pain. Flexibility is also important in certain sports specific movements and skills such as hiking out on sailboats and moving quickly from side to side of the boat during tacking maneuvers. Furthermore, flexibility decreases the chance of muscle and tendon strains and ligament sprains while lifting the heavy boats and gear.

Sailing is a physically demanding sport where competitors may be on the water for 5-8 hours continuously.

Program Suggestions:

Four factors should be considered for any fitness program to be effective. First, the *frequency of exercise* should be on average of three to five times per week. Secondly, the *intensity* or effort expended, should be appropriate for the age level and skill level of each person. A program which is too strenuous, may cause injury while a program which is too light, may not provide much benefit. Next, one should consider the *duration* or length of time spent doing exercises. It has been suggested that a minimum of 40 minutes per workout session is recommended for any substantial results to occur. Finally, the *mode* of exercise or what type of equipment to use becomes a consideration in any given program. Equipment which is easy to find, such as stairs, is recommended.

Since most sailing programs meet several times per week, it is easy to add an exercise component early each day for 15-30 minutes. Forty minutes of exercise per session may take up too much program time, but, extra swimming and running during games may help add more time and diversity to the general physical fitness program. Sailors might increase the intensity of their workout depending upon how old they are and they may choose to add a variety of activities to their daily routine. The main objective in working with children is to make it seem like fun.

To enhance one's performance, whether it be in golf, running, skiing, or sailing, certain sports specific factors should be taken into consideration prior to designing a fitness program. To maximize performance in sailing for instance, it is recommended that a program consists of *aerobic activity, weight training and stretching*.

Cardiovascular activity such as running or swimming can be included at the beginning of almost every program day right before the daily chalk talk. *Strength* can be improved in the abdominal, leg and upper body arm areas using just the body and very little other equipment. This added strength will help build muscles for hiking out in heavier wind conditions and maintain endurance during longer events. It is important to remember, what may be difficult for one person, may be easy for another. There is no magical number of how much or how little exercise to do. To experience an increase in muscular strength, maximum effort is required. For those who lack the muscular strength in the beginning to perform these exercises, they may modify the exercise to enable them to be performed. Those with less strength can modify these exercises slightly to enable them be performed. Here are some exercises which are easy to do in any program to build strength.

1. *Leg Strength*:

Running up and down stairs is not only good for the legs, but it also is a great cardiovascular workout. Any set of stairs will work for this.

Another superb exercise for strengthening the legs is lunges. Start with both feet pointing forward and hands at your sides. Take one step out approximately 3-4 shoe lengths and bend the back knee until it almost touches the ground (your front knee will be bent as well) and then come straight back up. Return to starting position and then alternate feet. Repeat the movement.

2. *Abdominal (stomach) strength*:

The simplest and most effective exercise is the crunch. Begin by laying flat on your back with knees bent at an angle and feet flat on the floor. Your hands should be placed behind your head with your elbows out. Slowly crunch the abdomianls by raising your shoulders off the ground, making sure to keep your chin and nose pointed toward the ceiling. Slowly return the shoulders to the ground. Repeat this action. It is important to exhale on the upward movement and inhale on the downward movement. Continue doing this until you feel a slight burn in the abdominals. Rest for 15-30 seconds and repeat the exercise again.

3. *Upper Body Strength*:

For the upper body there are two exercises which can improve one's muscular strength as well as endurance. Each exercise uses the individual's own body weight as resistance.

A. *Military push-ups increase the strength of the pectorals (chest), deltoids (shoulders) and triceps (back of arm).* To perform these push-ups, the individual should start on a surface free of any foreign objects. Lay flat on the stomach with the hands placed slightly wider than shoulder width. Keeping the back flat, have the individual push their body weight upwards. Do not fully lock the elbows at the top of the motion. Slowly, descend to the point where the elbows are bent at a 90 degree angle and then drive the body upwards once again. The exercise may be modified by placing the knees on the ground. This is to enable those who lack upper body strength to perform the exercise.

B. *Military pull-ups work the latissimus dorsi (back) and biceps (front of arm).* There are two basic grips that are used while performing pull-ups. The overhand (palms facing away from the body) and the underhand (palms facing towards the body). Alternating the grip may produce the best results. The bar should be high enough to allow the individual to hang freely when the knees are bent. Hands should be shoulder width apart. Slowly, pull the body upward to the point where the chin is above the bar, then slowly descend to the starting position and repeat the motion.

I recommend starting with two sets of each exercise. Try to do as many repetitions as possible, and progressively increase the set number to three while still performing the maximum repetitions the body can do without becoming too fatigued.

Finally, to maximize flexibility and minimize the potential for injury, it is important to *stretch* before and after a physical workout. The following stretches are recommended:

1. *Back and Hamstring Stretch:* While lying on your back, pull one leg towards your chest and hold. Keep the opposite leg as straight as possible. Lower the leg and repeat the motion with the other leg.

2. *Quadriceps:* While standing, bend one knee and place the heel of that foot at the base of the buttocks. Hold the top of the one foot with the opposite hand and gently pull your foot toward your buttock. Perform this action on both legs.

There are several important factors to remember while stretching. 1) Maintain normal breathing throughout the stretch. 2) Hold each stretch for twenty to thirty seconds. 3) Do not bounce or jerk while stretching. The motion should be controlled and gradual.

Sports Injuries:

As with every physical activity, there is always a chance of injury. The best way of avoiding a sports injury is by using preventive techniques. Although sailing is considered to be a non-contact sport (between people), injuries may still happen. Among the less serious of these are the traditional bumps, scrapes, and bruises which occur to everyone no matter how experienced. Small children tend to get their fingers pinched in their tiller extensions or more seriously, get their hands squashed between their boat and the dock as they reach to stop a boat. Heads are sometimes bumped by the boom as it swings from side to side. And finally, toes are stubbed while getting in and out of the boat. Most of these injuries hurt, but they are not serious and can be treated with a few bandaids and *TLC* (tender loving care).

However, there are some sports injuries which are far more critical. It has been shown in research studies, that the highest incident of sports deaths come from *heat-stroke*. While this may not seem possible on the water of cooler harbors such as on the west or northwest coasts, the southern harbors often find temperatures climbing to 90 degrees or higher with an 80% humidity level making four hours of sailing quite uncomfortable for almost anyone. Dehydration, lack of food and fatigue may all combine to increase the chances for serious injury and poor performance. For this reason, it is imperative for all sailors, especially young ones, to bring along water bottles and to constantly hydrate themselves. Water bottles can be secured in just about any boat, and parents should insist upon them as much as sunscreen, sunglasses and hats. In addition to water, on longer sailing days, quick energy food should be brought along to keep the blood sugar levels high. Plastic sacks can be filled with a child's favorite healthy snack. You might watch out for soft foods which will only get squished in the bottom of the boat.

As with any athletic activity, it is important to have a first aid kit available for emergencies. The following items are recommended:

1. Adhesive bandages (small and large sizes)
2. Antiseptic (for burns, stings, bites and rashes)
3. Ammonia Capsules (smelling salts)—Not to be used if any indication of a neck injury since it may cause a violent head jerk which could cause more spinal injury.

4. Aspirin/non-aspirin
5. Elastic wraps (ace Bandages)
6. Instant ice packs
7. Gauze pads
8. Adhesive tape
9. Any medication the child may need (asthma, antibiotics, etc.) should be given to the program director at the beginning of the day with a note of authorization and how to use it.
10. If in an earthquake zone, enough food and water for three days for each child as well as blankets, battery operated radio and flashlights.

Conclusion:

In order to maximize one's ability to compete, a fitness program must be in place several weeks before the actual event. It is not enough to work out one or two weeks prior to a regatta and think that any major good will come from it. It takes at least three or four weeks, or more, of solid preparation to be in top form. So it is important to plan ahead for competition (**see Chapter 7 Sports Psychology**) and physical fitness should be considered part of that planning schedule.

Finally, fitness does not just mean working out for hours each program day. Total fitness should become a lifestyle. Children can be taught that a proper diet (low in unsaturated fats), exercise and adequate rest is essential to one's total health. But true fitness is more than just being physically fit with exercise and diet. It is also being emotionally sound. Probably the most important factor of an overall fitness program is to enjoy the activity in which you are engaged in. People will only participate in an activity if it is enjoyable, so any fitness program must by fun. Children as well as adults need variety in their day in order to keep focused. A varied program of recreation and physical fitness can be part of a total fitness program which can be enjoyed for years to come.

A resource book to help sailors develop good physical and mental skills is:
   Mental and Physical Fitness for Sailing *- Alan Beggs, John Derbyshire, & Sir John Whitmore 1993*

CHAPTER NINE
AN INSTRUCTOR'S VIEW

The typical sailing instructor has come up through the ranks of being a junior sailor for many summers. Although some instructors may be in their 20s or 30s and bring with them a wealth of education experience, most are considerably younger. Most have an impressive resume filled with practical on the water experience. but far less classroom based experience. Program curriculums vary by location, so parents should check out the program quality issues discussed in **Chapter 2**.

It is my editorial opinion that parents need to occasionally be reminded that learning to sail is a voluntary recreational activity. Classes are taught through organized programs throughout the country, many of which are conducted through yacht clubs. These programs aim to teach the sailing to the community in order to share the sport with as many people as possible. Instructors are trained for many years, but they are not professional educators. They are hired to teach a loved skill and are not paid to baby-sit children or deal with children who have unique disciplinary needs. Parents need to be reminded that sailing programs are not as structured as a regular academic school and instructors are not usually well prepared to deal with exceptional behavioral problems. Try not to leave a child who has special needs all day in a program without asking the program director whether they are equipped to deal with these issues.

An important contribution a parent can make to their child's sailing education, is to visit the program and see for him/herself just what a typical day is like. For example, one summer we had a child who just refused to put sunscreen on his face even though all of the instructors and the life guard reminded him. When that child received a bad sunburn, the parents were furious with the staff and threatened to pull the child from the program. I remember talking with the staff and it was determined that the child would require a one to one instructor-student ratio in order to effectively solve the problem. Although this was a serious problem for the family, the parents were advised that greater personal responsibility was mandatory. The staff was alerted to keep reminding the child to put on the sunscreen, but it was expected that the parents would make sure that it was applied at home before he came to the program.

During another summer, a child found herself miserable during her first few days in class because she felt that everyone else could rig and unrig their boat independently by the end of the second day except her. Based on what their daughter said when she came home, both parents complained to the program director that the staff seemed to ignore her individual needs. After investigating the actual situation, it was determined that the young girl was brand new to the program and indeed some of the students were more skilled in rigging then she was. The staff discovered this, and had planned to independently work with her later in the week. But before they had a chance to discuss this on the second day of her session, she left early for a doctor's appointment making it difficult for the staff to take her aside individually. Further, her parents had asked her to unrig her boat before she was picked up. Since she could not get special attention to do this, she left her boat sitting in the water and left with her parents. She missed some of the important experiences the second day which could have helped her catch up with the rest of the class. Both parents expected that their daughter would have an easy time adapting to the program, yet they unknowingly kept her from fitting in with the other children. They could not understand why a staff member was not available to give special consideration to their child, but they were not forthcoming in discussing reasonable options in how to help their child.

Parents need to remember that a program is staffed with one instructor per 5-8 kids. Any special considerations should become the parent's responsibility if for no other reason then the fact that staff is attending to many things at once on and off the water. To help you understand what a typical program day and instructor is like, I have included the following interview.

Jason Artof was Head Instructor at Del Rey Yacht Club in Marina Del Rey for several years during the 1990s before graduating college and becoming a mechanical engineer. Most recently he has coached Laser sailing for University of California Irvine (UCI) and taught adult sailing at the UC Irvine sail base. He has won several major championship regattas including the *US SAILING/ROLEX Junior Championships* in 1989 (doublehanded with Peter Wells), The *US SAILING Singlehanded Championship* semi finals and the *US SAILING/ROLEX Junior Championship* (singlehanded) semi finals in 1992 and the *Capri 14.2 Nationals* in 1992 and 1993. He was also selected to sail in the *NAUTICA/US SAILING Youth Championships* sailed in Gulfport, Mississippi; Milwaukee Wisconsin; Alamitos Bay, California; and

Greenwich, Connecticut as well as selected as part of the *Los Angeles Youth Sailing Team* which participated in Nagoya Japan in 1989. Jason sailed competitively in college as a member of the UCI Sailing Team. Sailing has been an important part of his life, even helping him to focus on a career path in engineering. After graduating, Jason continues to actively teach as well as compete in small boats. His background and experience qualifies him as a good representative of what an average sailing instructor's day is like throughout the country.

Del Rey Yacht Club's junior program ranks as one of the finest in the country. The program has trained major youth champions as well as becoming the proving ground for many of today's best youth instructors. The youth sailing curriculum is considered a large program by today's standards with over 70 students per week attending classes. There are smaller programs offered at yacht clubs and community sailing centers throughout the country. Some might meet once per week for several weeks while others might meet every day. What the following interview with Jason illustrates are some general truths that can apply to both large and small programs no matter where they are found.

1. **How long have you been sailing?**

I began sailing when I was 7 1/2 years old. I wanted to begin the program, but I admit that it scared me for a few seasons. I needed to get used to the wind and what that did to the boat.

2. **How long have you been an instructor?**

I became an instructor's assistant when I was in 10th grade. I must have been 15 years old at the time. I didn't want to stop taking sailing classes, but I also wanted to work and had taken enough sailing clinics from other instructors to know something about teaching. The next year I was an instructor and remained one for two seasons. I was made Head Instructor, after my first year of college.

3. What kind of training did you need to become Head Instructor of a major program?

To become an instructor in my program it is mandatory to take an instructor training class, and the best class available is the **US SAILING** Instructor training. I became Level 1 certified. I have also taken three years of CISA (California International Sailing Association) seminars which offer some of the best teaching from some of the best teachers around. There are Olympians and coaches from all over that participate in this training. Finally, since I traveled all around the country in the **US SAILING** Championships, I was fortunate to participate in seminars offered for each regatta. Finally, the training I received as a college sailor on the UCI championship team helped me improve my own teaching drills and skills. All of this training helped me understand what is good and bad teaching. I remember being a kid and the fear I felt trying to master the boat. I try hard to help others get over that fear.

4. What does a typical day look like to you during the summer program?

Our program runs 4 days per week (Mon.-Thurs.) and begins a 8:45 AM and ends at 4:00 PM. Kids come early in the morning and take about an hour to rig their boats. Since it is summer, some kids straggle in a little later and we tell everyone to meet on the patio near the pool at 9:45 AM for what we call a chalk talk or instruction using the black board.

At this chalk talk, everyone warms up with some sort of exercise and perhaps a few laps around the clubhouse. Many of the kids grumble about this and try to convince the instructors that this is not a PE class, but I feel that it is important to strengthen and condition the body even during the summer. After the exercises, we usually break into skill level groups with beginners, intermediates and advanced sailors breaking off with a different instructor. Sometimes the entire group will be doing the same thing such as sailing to the park or working on a relay race or sailing project, and groups will not be formed. If groups are formed, then each instructor will discuss a new point of sailing with their students during individual chalk talks after the main one.

Kids will then go out on their boats and work on certain drills or sail to a part of the harbor for some fun and recreation. We always have two chase boats available and are working on getting a third so that each group can actually sail in a different place of the harbor. During the last few summers, we must combine the beginning and intermediate groups more often than I would like.

Everyone sails until approximately 12:00-12:30 and we then sail back for lunch. Some of the kids buy their lunch and some bring it. We relax and eat. After digesting, we break into groups again with the better sailors going back out to sail and race for the next two hours while the less skilled sailors go to the swimming pool to work on conditioning and swimming skills. At approximately 2:30-3:00 everyone sails back to unrig their boats and finish the day swimming.

A few times per week, students can remain until 7:00-8:00 PM and race in evening races which are sponsored by different yacht clubs in the harbor. Parents are encouraged to come and support their kids during these late afternoon races.

5. **What is the biggest problem you have had to encounter as an instructor?**

Of course I've had the scary problems of kids getting knocked on the head with their booms or cuts on their fingers. We have first aid kits around, and our life guard is always available. All of the instructors are trained in CPR and First Aid and we have a full-time staff person in the office to call paramedics for any emergencies. Fortunately, we have never had a major incident, but we try to be alert all of the time.

The worst problems we have are behavioral. Sometimes kids come to the program and are just rebelling about doing anything. These kids can sit around and complain all day no matter what we have them doing. This makes it bad for the other kids who really want to be there. If kids do not want to come to a volunteer program, then maybe they shouldn't. Once kids get bored, the instructors can never get them back for that day. It is just better to keep everyone busy and not let them get bored. It is hard keeping this energy up all day if kids begin to complain.

Other problems we seem to have are kids teasing other kids. Since everyone is around water all day, sometimes the teasing can get out of hand. Our instructors need to keep alert all of the time to enforce standards. If we forget to communicate these standards the kids seem to push the limits more and more. It is important for parents to help their kids understand that sailing is a volunteer activity and that there are certain rules which should be followed or else the child will be asked to leave.

I will also admit that I have had some problems with other instructors. When I ask them to do something and they don't do it, I have to talk with the parents about it or even my own Director. I can't be everywhere at once. One summer I had some problems with a staff member who was more difficult to discipline then the kids. Obviously, we are not rehiring that person this summer.

6. What is it like to work with brand new beginning sailors. Can you relate to them?

I like working with new kids if they are enthusiastic. I know that they are frightened of new things, but enthusiasm is contagious and makes it fun for everyone. In our program we give nicknames to some of the kids, and we look forward to these kids coming to class. Even if they have a hard time learning how to sail, they will be the best one's later. Probably the worst thing about working with beginners is when they are too young to really become part of the group and they just cannot understand what is going on.

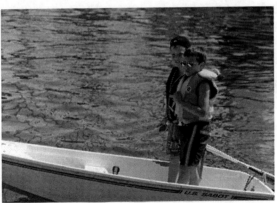

Many programs put two beginners together in a boat to give them confidence.

7. What is the most important quality an instructor should have on order to work with beginning sailors?

Patience! It takes a lot of patience to work with kids and help them have fun. A good instructor does not have to be the best racer, but they have to be able to work well with kids and keep them enthusiastic.

8. How do you handle discipline problems? What is a common technique you make use of?

We have problems every year with kids who push limits of everyone's patience. We have developed a code of standards that kids and their parents must sign before coming to the program. This list includes rules for where the kids can go while in the program, how they should act with others and so forth. However, one year we had more problems with stealing, bad language and general disrespect towards both instructors and other kids. We developed an even stricter set of standards to sign and each parent was informed that the child would be sent home if these rules were violated. It seems simple, but some parents were not aware that their children were causing any problems, so we informed them early about such concerns.

The smaller problems are usually handled by taking the student out of the class and asking them to have a time out with the life guard. Usually this works, although, sometimes the child likes sitting at the pool more than sailing and they begin to find ways to get in trouble. We also have kids helping to clean up and do work or extra exercises when they have a bad day. We must be flexible since everyday is different. There is always a challenge.

One thing we definitely do not do is use any form of physical punishment with the child.

9. How do you handle fear in young kids?

I was afraid of sailing when I was young, and I know that the best way of handling fear is to encourage the child. Sometimes having an older sailor work with a younger one helps. Sometimes taking the child out of the group and working solo with them works.

Positive feedback works well with fearful kids. If they are worried about the wind blowing, get their minds onto something else and encourage them into getting into the boat. When they see that other people are having fun, they may get their courage up and try to overcome the fear. In our program we also have everyone practice capsizing their boats so they can actually experience the worst thing that can happen. The more they do that, the less fear they will have. They gain more control.

What doesn't work is yelling or embarrassing the child. We don't do that in our program and neither should parents.

10. **What tips can you give parents to help their kids in a sport such as sailing?**

As I was saying about fear, yelling and humiliating the child is not right. Kids have feelings, and parents should not make them feel badly. Parents have to realize that sailing is difficult even though it may look easy. I suggest that parents get on the small boats with their children and see what it is like. In our program we have a race which encourages this. It is called the junior senior race, and kids sail a relay type race with their parents. The winning team is one where both the young sailor and the beginning parent sailor actually completes the race course. Kids have a chance to yell out encouragement to their parents.

Another tip I can give is to encourage parents to be at the races when their kids are competing. Not everyone wins, and having a parent there makes you feel good when you have had a bad day. Besides, if you do win, it feels really good to have a parent there to greet you at the dock. In our program, we make a party out of race day, and we bring over kids to act as a rooting section even if they are not racing. Parents are then encouraged to come back to the clubhouse for a bar-B-Q. This has become a tradition, and kids can unrig their boats with their parents there to help. Get involved.

Also, sometimes winning championships at too young an age can be hard on a kid. Their expectations are too high and they feel that they are under a lot of pressure to perform. Be careful about pushing your child too hard and too soon.

11. What tips can you give a kid to help them develop their skills?

Have fun! If you don't have fun, why do it? Practice and don't get discouraged. Get your friends to sail with you. It is not fun to sail alone, and if your friends sail, it feels like summer all of the time. You can only get better if you practice. Also, keep your body physically fit. Races are lost because people get tired. Drink lots of water and take a snack out for long races. Keep your head clear and focused.

12. Finally, you have traveled the country in competitive sailing. What has sailing really given to you? How has it influenced your life?

Well, it has given me an outlet and a chance to be competitive so when things didn't go well in one area of my life, I could turn to sailing. It made me feel better about myself as I grew up. It has given me a good tan —yes I wear sunscreen—and something to do each summer since I was 7 1/2 years old. Sailing has sculpted my mind and helped me think about things in a different way. I ask a lot of questions about how things work. You might say that I think of things in an engineering sort of way and I did this a long time before I decided to become an engineer. I have always thought of things in a large-scale sort of way, like asking questions about the clouds and the weather and how all of this will effect my performance.

At one point of my life I was going to design boats. Fast boats. When I was in high school I remember doing a semester term project on sailing. My teachers did not know how to sail, so they were very impressed without really knowing what I was talking about. My early sailing experience allowed me to conceptualize how wind and water works to make a boat go faster. Eventually I began working with fluid mechanics and became interested in how the heart works. Today I make heart valves.

I've been able to travel a lot with my sailing, and I always have something to do when I get there. I like to be active. Anywhere there is water there are boats. I like to travel near water.

Sailing probably helped me get into the college of my choice since I was on a varsity sailing team. My resume looked good when I applied and even though there was no money in sailing, the university supported its sailors with extra help getting classes, extra tutorial services and extra guidance counseling which was a great help to me.

CHAPTER TEN
SAILING
ORGANIZATIONS

Sometimes called the alphabet soup, the organizational map of United States sailing moves from the national level of organizations to the local region, each with its own alphabet description of labels. Because I am from Southern California, I will discuss these labels as they apply to our specific region, but there are regions for each specific area of the country which will apply directly to you, the reader.

International Organization:

In 1996, The International Yacht Racing Union (IYRU) changed its name to the **International Sailing Federation (ISAF)** and today is the official governing body of the sport of sailing. They are responsible for *developing a uniform set of racing rules and measurement standard* for the entire sport throughout the world. The need for standards came about as a result of a century of arbitrary and individual racing rules developed by each locality. Today 122 member nations make up the ISAF and have agreed upon a set of rules and standards that are constant throughout the world. 76 recognized classes are standardized including the smallest boat, the Optimist Dinghy to the largest maxi sailboat. You can find information regarding the ISAF at: *http://www.sailing.org*.

National Organization:

The *National Governing* body for sailing in the United States is called The **United States Sailing Association (US SAILING)**. The basic function of **US SAILING** is to *administer racing, education and training programs for all sailors and sailing instructors, develop and administer race officer recognition programs, and conduct certain US SAILING Championships*. Except for a small paid staff which is located in Newport Rhode Island, **US SAILING** is run by volunteers who have developed an exceptional love for the sport. They are willing to devote much of their time and money to help administer the many programs this organization has become famous for including most of the safety and race management programs which affect our youth.

US SAILING is divided into ten *Areas* or *Councils* that are broken into 37 regional sailing associations. Each Area is designated by a letter of the alphabet. Letters A-H and J and K represent each of these areas. *Area Directors* are selected for each area and serve on a *Council of Sailing Associations (CSA)* All Areas have regular Council meetings where important matters of the specific region are discussed including the specifics for **US SAILING** ladder events. The Area Directors are asked to be on the **US SAILING** *Association's Board of Directors* and they attend meetings (especially the annual **US SAILING** meeting held each year in October) to discuss the direction American sailing is going. For example, the Area J Council (the Area I sail out of) Director will report all of our regional concerns at that meeting. This type of regional direction makes sailing one of the most democratically run sports in America.

US SAILING Areas:

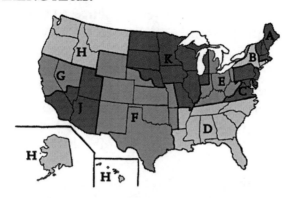

As shown on the US SAILING 2002 website

US SAILING Councils
*As described in the **US SAILING** 2002 website*

Area A
Mass Bay SA
Narragansett Bay SA
Southern Mass SA
Northeast SA

Area B
Central New York YRA
Eastern Conn. SA
Eastern Long Island SA
Great South Bay YRA
Hudson River YRA
YRA of Long Island Sound

Area C
Barnegat Bay YRA
Chesapeake Bay YRA
Mid-Atlantic YRA
North Jersey YRA

Area D
Dixie Inland YRA
Florida SA
Gulf YA
South Atlantic YRA

Area E
Detroit Regional YA
Inter-Lake YRA
Lake Huron YA
Lake YRA
Ohio Valley YA

Area F
Central States SA
SA of Intermountain Lakes
Texas SA

Area G
SBRA of Northern California
YRA of San Fransisco Bay

Area J
Southern Calif. YA
YRA of Southern Calif.

Area H
Hawaii YRA
Pacific International YA
North Rockies SA

Area K
Inland Lake YA
Lake Michigan SRF
Lake Superior YA
Midwest SA

In addition to the Council of Sailing Associations, sailors have organized associations and councils that have common interests. These groups serve as communication conduits for specific issues in the sport and are linked together through **US SAILING**. Currently there are 10 major interest groups.

American Model Yachting Association
Community Sailing Council.
Council of Sailing Associations
Inter-collegiate Sailing Association
Interscholastic Sailing Association
Multihull Council
National Offshore Council
One-Design Council
Sailor Athlete Advisory Council
US Windsurfing Association

Besides the specific Councils and Associations which make up the main structure of **US SAILING**, the organization is broken into several committees including special committees for Olympic Yachting Race Administration, Inshore and Offshore Sailing, General Services, and Training. There are even special committees devoted to sailors with special needs, legal and government concerns, and international yachting all working through **US SAILING**. In addition, **US SAILING** helps to select the official US Olympic Sailing Team members. Thus, any changes in the racing rules, safety at sea programs or even new developments in instructor certification, are all coordinated through this highly visible national organization.

US SAILING Memebership:

To sail in any of the **US SAILING** Championship regattas, or to even attend many of the programs or to be on any of the special committees, a person must be a member of the organization. Membership costs in 2002 were as follows:

$15 Youth (U.S. resident under 21)	$50 Individual
$75 Family, Contributing	$90 for 2 years
$130 for 2 years	$120 for 3 years
$180 for 3 years	

Members receive special bonuses such as gift certificates and a subscription to *Sailing World*.

Because **US SAILING** has contributed so much to the sport, the organization encourages sailors to become involved early in their introduction to the sport. Everyone wins when the participants of the sport act to support it. Junior sailors are encouraged to join as either an individual youth member or as a family member.

US SAILING has also initiated a special *Junior Golden Anchor* program aimed at youth organizations, scholastic and collegiate teams and clubs, community sailing programs and junior yacht clubs. As described in the 2002 **US SAILING** Website. "The Golden Anchor Program is designed to give more benefits to your members and your organization...whether yours is a yacht club, sailing association, One Design Class Association, or community sailing program. In short, any organization involved with sailing can take advantage of what Golden Anchor has to offer." In 2002 membership dues were $12 (instead of $15) for a junior; $40 for individual (instead of $50) and $60 for a family (compared to $75). Coaches, faculty advisors, parents and even local merchants can support junior sailing by joining **US SAILING** at the Golden Anchor (for adults)

A sport is only as good as the participants in it, and the philosophy of encouraging responsibility in our junior sailing participants seems to be working quite well. These kids seem to be developing a good attitude about the sport they have chosen.

In addition to the genuine help in running most of the important sailing activities in the United States, **US SAILING**. Beginning in 1994, the organization has affiliated with *Sailing World Magazine* and offers a free subscription to the magazine as part of the membership package. They also publish quarterly, *Junior Sailor*, exclusively for **US SAILING's** Junior Sailors. For a young sailor and their family, these magazines are terrific ways of keeping involved with the sport.

Finally, for information regarding ways to fund a specific program, campaign, or ways to develop training or special community based programs in your area, you might want to contact **US SAILING Foundation** (USSF). This organization has dispensed more than $2,500,00 in grants and is the motor behind the U.S. Sailing Team as well as development of sportsmanship values such as the **US SAILING** Rescue Medal. Another way a person might get involved in the sailing world without putting in much time, is to consider calling USSF and offer a donation for their endowment fund. USSF is a tax-free, non profit organization recognized by the IRS under 501(c)(3) and donations could qualify as a tax deduction for the donor to the extent permitted by law. Talk this over with your tax advisor.

For more information about **US SAILING** and its programs, contact:

> **US SAILING**
> PO Box 1260
> 15 Maritime Drive
> Portsmouth, RI 02871-0907
>
> Membership 1-800-USSAIL1
> Phone 401-683-0800
> Fax 401-683-0840
> E-Mail info@ussailing.org
> website: http://www.ussailing.org

Area Organization:

As mentioned above, **US SAILING** is comprised of 10 *Areas*, each headed by its own director who reports to the national Board of Directors. Our family lives in Southern California and sails in what is called **Area J**. If we lived in Florida, we would be part of **Area D** and if we sailed out of San Francisco (Northern California) we would be a part of **Area G**. Each area is then divided into local harbor regions made up of individual yacht clubs located in that particular area. These local areas are called *Associations*. I sail out of Del Rey Yacht Club (**DRYC**) which is located in Marina Del Rey and is part of an Association of yacht clubs called *The Association Of Santa Monica Bay Yacht Clubs* (**ASMBYC**). The Pacific Mariner's Yacht Club (**PCYC**) is located in the Channel Islands/ Santa Barbara area and is a member of *The Association Of Santa Barbara Channel Yacht Clubs* (**ASBCYC**).

Each local Association may have its own ladder elimination races to determine champion level competitors who will continue on to the **US SAILING** Championships. These Association winners will then compete in Area elimination races, the winner going to the final national level championship. For example, there is a youth event sailed each year to determine the best singlehanded, doublehanded and multiple crewed boat champions, and competitors sail to win either the *Smythe Trophy* for singlehanded sailors, the *Bemis Trophy* for doublehanded sailors or the *Sears Trophy* for triple- handed sailors. In Area J there are five separate harbor associations. **ASMBYC** and **ASBCYC** are two of those five. Our son Jason competed for the double-handed *Bemis Trophy* back in 1989 and won the local harbor elimination, making him eligible to sail for the Area J elimination. He and his partner, Peter Wells, also won that regatta and were then sent back to Greenwich, Connecticut where they sailed the finals at Indian Harbor Yacht Club (**IHYC**). They won that regatta and were award the **US SAILING**/ROLEX *Junior Championship* for doublehanded sailing and were the winners of the *Bemis Trophy*. A few years later Jason won the **Area J** elimination's for the *Smythe Trophy* and the *O'Day Trophy* leading to the US Singlehanded Sailing Championship and went to the **US SAILING** Finals for both. Besides conducting the elimination level races for these championships, local Harbor Associations often support junior sailing by offering extra training/coaching as well as funding for many of the young competitors who are working so hard to succeed at their sport.

Yacht Club Organization:
It is not always a requirement to be affiliated with a yacht club or Harbor Association in order to sail. But, sailing/yacht clubs do offer something special to the general boating community. Boating might be considered a lifestyle that encourages friendly cooperation and sportsmanship among its participants, and boaters who

meet other boaters may become instant friends. Yacht clubs help to form a common interest bond between people adding to the quality of social and educational activities. There are well over 2,200 such clubs spread across the United States, and several thousand other clubs throughout the world. Some of these organizations maintain a roster of only a few members and no actual clubhouse facility. Members only get together for an occasional meeting at a local restaurant and all other functions are on member's boats. Dues may be as little as $40 per year for such a club. Then there are other yacht clubs which are far more elaborate in their facilities and may offer swimming pools and restaurants as well as gas docks, local anchorage and immediate help when needed while cruising. These clubs may hire staff including club managers and dock captains along with full time junior activity directors. Big clubs and little clubs often contribute equally to their harbor. Although different in staff and facility availability, most clubs belonging to a Harbor Association, such as **ASMBYC**, will be involved with yachting and boating activities and offer help in race management and safety education along with a full calendar of racing and social events. Some clubs even offer reciprocal privileges to members of other clubs so that these members might travel throughout the world and find a gracious welcome mat laid out for them.

Your child may be offered a special membership in the club he or she is taking lessons at. If you as a parent are not affiliated with a club, look into the program your child is in. There may be a special membership program for you as well. As a parent of a junior sailor, consider finding a program and club for you and your family. It will add to the enjoyment of this sport.

YRUs and SAs:

Individual yacht clubs within each harbor are connected by regional yachting associations also called **YRUs (yacht racing unions)** or **SAs (sailing associations)** though most of the boats participating in any major regatta are usually too small to be considered *yachts*. Southern California has two different YRUs governing the area. *Del Rey Yacht Club* and *Westlake Yacht Club* are both a part of one such organization called *The Southern California Yachting Association* (**SCYA**) which conducts its own regatta (Midwinters), holds meetings where yacht club delegates discuss problems, and administers training seminars on race management and Safety at Sea. Another club organization or Yacht Racing Union connects clubs together which have specific facilities such as dining rooms and junior programs and which are considered to be nonprofit, that is, owned and operated by the members rather than for a profit centered corporation. **YRUSC** is the Southern California chapter of this organization and conducts club management programs where clubs can share their successes and discuss management problems and other issues related to the overall boating community.

These organizations also help to support various boater lobbying organizations which may influence Federal and State laws affecting all boaters. For example, there was a successful effort to help overturn a Federal Boat User Tax on vessels over 15 feet. There is also an effort to forestall a recent Coast Guard requirement which will make it mandatory that sailing instructors, even those on small lakes, pass and be licensed to operate large for hire passenger boats, something which will instantly dissolve most of the community and club sailing programs in our country. Running a 15 ft. chase boat is not the same as operating a 100 ft.

charter boat, but the licensing requirements are being interpreted the same.

Finally, there are groups that have formed to assist the YRUs and SAs in developing certain mission statements. One special such group in California is called the *Southern California Youth Yacht Racing Association* (**SCYYRA**) and works directly with SCYA to develop and enrich youth sailing programs in the Southern California area. This organization sponsors a number of junior regattas, identifies potential champion sailors, and works with **US SAILING** to improve the quality of junior programs throughout the region. **SCYYRA** also co-sponsors a special clinic called the **CISA** clinic held each year at Alamitos Bay Yacht Club in California. **CISA** (*California International Sailing Organization*) was established in 1971 as a non profit group whose mission is to help identify and develop the talents of youth sailors throughout the country. Other such youth organizations are in full operation throughout various regions of the country. Get in touch with your local association and find out how you might become more involved in your region.

So, now you have an overview of the alphabet soup organizations which keeps the motor driving in this sport called sailing. There is an interesting tradition that goes along with the yachting community. Every year, at a prearranged time in the spring, yacht clubs around the country celebrate the beginning of the yachting season in a ceremony called *Opening Day*. On this day, members and their families along with delegates from many of the local and regional boating organizations, get together wearing their prescribed uniforms, shoot off small canons or shotguns, raise burgees (yacht club flags), recite prayers of thanks for a chance to participate in this unique recreational sport, and then eat themselves silly. On the east coast and in the Midwestern lake regions, the yachting season is only a few months long, with ice and snow affecting all but the heartiest ice sailors in the winter. On the West Coast and in the south, sailors delight in their sport all year around. But everyone agrees, "There is nothing- absolutely nothing- half so much doing, as simply messing about in boats...or with boats...In or out of 'em, it doesn't matter." *Kenneth Grahame, The Wind in the Willows (1908)*. And why not begin when you are young.

Chapter Eleven
Youth Championship Racing/Training

US SAILING Events:
Here is a listing of the most important youth sailing events sponsored by **US SAILING**. There are some very specific eligibility rules for these races, so be sure to check with **US SAILING** to determine if the criterion for sailing is in fact established.

U.S.A. Junior Olympic National Sailing Championship
(originally named Youth Champs)
Applicants must be members of **US SAILING** and cannot have reached their 20th birthday in the year of the race. The **US SAILING** Youth Committee selects participants based on the entry form and resume presented. Since this is not a ladder elimination event, only the most competitive and skilled singlehanded, doublehanded sailors in the United States are chosen. It is recommended that sailors who want to be accepted into this elite event sail throughout the year in many high level regattas and include an advanced racing clinic such as CISA or the Oyster Bay Sailing Foundation Clinic to their resume.

The singlehanded sailors selected sail lasers (recently also a radial class is selected) while the doublehanded sailors sail in 420s but have sailed Laser IIs, One design 14s and other exciting boats in the past. **US SAILING** decides which boat will be used for this event, and holds that boat for at least five years. In 1997 a developmental 470 fleet was added to encourage talented sailors to try their hand at an actual Olympic boat. In 1998 the Europe dinghy was added for singlehanded women who want to test their skill on an Olympic class boat. Coaches are allowed on the water, and may coach up to the prepatory gun, but may not coach after. While on the water, coaches are asked to help the race committee with safety issues if necessary.

Winners of each division can qualify (if age eligible) to compete in the International Sailing Federation World Youth Sailing Championships. The United States has had several World Champions emerge out of an extremely talented field of youth sailors.

As many as 150 youths participate in this race that is held at a different yacht club each year. There are a limited number of charter boats available, so early filing of charter requests is important once you are accepted. Send in your application early, and a list of accepted competitors will be listed in early May on the **US SAILING** website.

Often times individual clubs will help defray the cost of transportation to this regatta for the sailor, although parents and family costs must be paid for individually. Housing arrangements are included in the cost of this regatta as well as food and entertainment. There is a **US SAILING Clinic** attached to all of the high level championship races that helps make just participating in these regattas something of an experience which cannot be duplicated. This event is usually sailed the third week of June and participants remain in the area for close to one week.

For more information on this event and to get an application, go to:

www.ussailing.org/youthchamps.

Coaches observing a congested startline at the Youth Champs.

U.S. Junior Singlehanded, Doublehanded, Triplehanded Championship

Sears Cup/Bemis and Smythe Trophies

This race is for sailors aged 13-18 who are members of US SAILING and all crew must be from the same yacht club or community sailing organization of a club recognized by the local YRA. The Sears Cup is sailed in a 3 person boat; The Bemis Trophy is sailed in a 2 person boat; The Smythe Trophy is sailed in a one person boat. Check the website for details on which boat is selected for the current year's championship.

Competitors qualify through ladder events organized by harbor associations and **US SAILING** areas. Currently, the top **two** winners of the Area Association eliminations are eligible to compete. Contact **US SAILING** (401-683-0800) for the name and number of your local ladder event organizer. Like the Youth Champs, this event is sailed at a different yacht clubs each year. Parents are invited to watch this event on provided spectator boats. The event is usually sailed during the third week of August and participants remain in the area for close to a week including the pre-race clinic. Coaches and parents may not interact with competitors after a pre-race warning is issued, and they may not be in direct contact until the end of the day. Spectator boats are always available for parents and coaches to watch from.

All boats are provided for. Housing and food arrangements are made for each child to stay with a family and these arrangements are mandatory. No child is allowed to be housed with his or her parent for this event. Area winners who are eligible for the finals are usually able to secure funding from their home club, Association, and/or Area. Check with your club or program director for details on how to secure funding.

U.S. Junior Women's Singlehanded Championship
Nancy Leiter Clagett Trophy
An open event for women under 19 years of age who are members of **US SAILING** and sailed in singlehanded boats (radial rigged lasers). Participation is by resume and application. This race is sailed in clubs throughout the United States and is sailed usually the beginning weeks of August. Ask about funding through your club and Association. Some charter boats are available if applied for early, but the best boats are usually brought from home. Parents are encouraged to participate on spectator boats if arrangements are made. Housing arrangements are made for each participant in case parents do not come.

U.S. Junior Women's Doublehanded Championship
Ida Lewis Trophy
An open event for women under 19 years of age who are members of **US SAILING** and currently sailed in doublehanded trapeze boats (420s). Participation is by resume and application. This race is sailed in clubs throughout the United States and is sailed usually the

beginning weeks of August. Ask about funding through your club and Association. Some charter boats are available if applied for early, but the best boats are usually brought from home. Parents are encouraged to participate on spectator boats if arrangements are made. Housing arrangements are made for each participant in case parents do not come.

U.S. Singlehanded Championship
O'Day Cup Trophy
Although this is not strictly a youth event, this popular regatta always encourages the best laser sailors to compete. Open to **US SAILING** members 16 years and older who qualify by ladder eliminations through their Association and Area. Qualification through **Area eliminations, intercollegiate sailing, high school sailing, women's, Youth or military**. The top area winners often are eligible for funding and boats are provided for the finals. Housing arrangements can be made through the regatta committee or competitors may stay with their families in local hotels.

U.S. Youth Mulithull Championships
Hoytt/Jolly Cup
An annual open event, currently sailed in the Hobie 16 for boy, girl, and mixed teams under 19 years of age in the year of the race. Winners will qualify for the ISAF Youth Worlds the next year.

Other Recognized Championships and Events:
Junior Match Racing Championship
Governors Cup Match Race
This is the premier youth match racing event in the country with participants invited by resume application submitted by various yacht clubs throughout the world. A

team consists of three people from each club whose members have reached their 15th birthday by the first day of racing and have not yet reached 20 years of age. The race is sailed in Santana 20 boats (or whatever the host club, Balboa Yacht Club, chooses). There are a limited number of slots for this race and teams compete for a berth in this prestigious regatta. The winning United States Team is invited to sail in the Coca-Cola Cup World Youth Match Racing Championships in Auckland, NZ. A successful youth program, King Harbor Yacht Club in Redondo Beach, California, has sent three teams to this event. Send a resume to request a team entry to:

Governor's Cup Chairman
Balboa Yacht Club
1801 Bayside Drive
Corona del Mar, CA 92625
(949) 673-3515
Fax (949) 673-8937

Clinics and Advanced Training:
There are several clinics and advanced racing seminars offered throughout the year. Two special ones are the CISA and Oyster Bay Sailing Foundation programs offered to the most talented youth sailors in the country.

Sailors at the CISA clinic work together to take out their boats. Sailors get to know eachother during this week of intense training.

CISA raises money for Olympic bound competitors and trains Olympic hopefuls. Established as a 501.c.3 non profit foundation in 1971, CISA promotes sailing through travel grants and support at the highest level of sailing giving more than $5 million dollars to worthy competitors since 1984. The CISA clinic is held each spring in Alamitos Bay California. Sailors apply to sail 29ers, 420s, CFJs, Europe, Lasers and Radial rigs. These competitors are treated to land and sea instruction by some of the world's best talents all brought together for this one special week during Spring Break. This clinic is open to all young sailors (most 16 years of age or older) who are selected by resume. Contact CISA in early winter for an application and information.

For Information regarding the **CISA** program and clinic contact:

Marilee Goyan c/o CISA
California International Sailing Association
P.O. Box 17992
Irvine, CA 92713-7992
http://www.cisasailing.org

The Oyster Bay Sailing Foundation also puts on an Advanced Racing Clinic at the US Merchant Marine Academy in King's Point N.Y. As with CISA, the top Olympian, collegiate sailors and coaches help young sailors refine their skills in Lasers, Radials, and club 420s. For more information contact:

Susie Trotman
(516) 367-3238
strotman@compuserve.com.

For information about junior programs in your area or on how you might become more involved with junior sailing contact:

Joni Palmer, Sailing Consultant
Assistant Director of Intercollegiate
Sailing
(410) 293-5615
jpalmer@usna.edu

For information about instructor training, community sailing opportunities or ways you might set up a program for junior sailing in your area, contact **US SAILING** direct.

US SAILING
PO Box 1260
15 Maritime Drive
Portsmouth, RI 02871-0907

Membership 1-800-USSAIL1
Phone (401) 683-0800
Fax (401) 683-0840
E-Mail info@ussailing.org

AFTERWORD

I hope that you have enjoyed reading this book as much I have enjoyed writing it. Since the first edition of this book appeared in 1994, I have spent even more hours on the dock talking to parents and kids who have become completely enthralled with the sport of sailing. In preparing the updates to this current edition, I realize how much can change in the details such as phone numbers and websites (there were no websites back in 1994), and yet there is a sense of constancy in the sport that is comforting. I know that there is more material here then readers can possibly absorb in a single reading, and I hope the book is used as a reference guide to be looked at over and over again. But in summary, I think that kids and parents may agree on how sailing, as a recreational activity, can enrich one's life.

A Final Word On Where Sailing May Lead:
Whether a family sails out of a big club or a small one, or out of a community sailing program sponsored by a school or park, the pure recreational activity of sailing brings special rewards. There is rarely a huge sports contract at the end of the game for any of us, but there are life lessons and enriching experiences that can transform a person in so many ways. Sailing can offer:

1. Acceptance to college.
2. A possible career path in sail making, nautical architecture and design or even engineering.
3. Development of teaching skills and a great summer job (and tan).
4. Travel opportunities to many regattas around the country and around the world.
5. A life long hobby which may extend well into adulthood.

For those readers who may wish to learn more about sailing, there is a nice comfortable way to do so by watching some of the many exciting videos which are available. Some of the better ones include a series put out by **US SAILING** titled *Learn To Sail Videos* with topics ranging from beginning sailing, to lines and knots, to sailing fast, or man overboard recovery. There are also some wonderful sailing videos available at your local marine store or marine catalog dealers including West Marine, Armchair Sailor, or Boat US. Surf the web and you will find many online sites that specialize in books and videos for sailors including *Amazon.com*. Contact your closest marine dealer and ask for a list of current videos and books and share the experience with your child.

This is the second edition of this book, and I hope to update again in a few years. This volume is intended to become an interactive work with increasing clarity and focus with each new printing. To accomplish this, I am asking that readers send in your experiences so that we might include new chapters with information that is updated and applicable to the changing world we live in. Drop us a line anytime, and we will be happy to respond with your comments.

Also, for those of you who wish establishing a sailing program in your area and do not know how to go about starting one, contact **US SAILING** with your questions. They will be glad to steer you in the right direction. There are many ways you can become an involved family in the sport of sailing. You just need to know where to begin.

We hope to hear from as many of you as possible regarding your successes.

The Center Press
PO Box 6936
Thousand Oaks, CA 91362
(818) 889-7071
Fax (818) 889-7072
center@centerbooks.com
http://www.centerbooks.com

Whether one boat or many boats, there is a trailer to move them from place to place.

INDEX